MAKING HUMAN RIGHTS WORK GLOBALLY

Anthony Woodiwiss

glasshouse press

London • Sydney • Portland, Oregon

First published 2003 by GlassHouse Press

Transferred to digital printing 2007
by GlassHouse Press
2 Park Square, Milton Park, Abingdon, Oxon, OX14 4RN

Simultaneously published in the USA and Canada
by GlassHouse Press
270 Madison Avenue, New York, NY 10016

The GlassHouse Press is an imprint of Cavendish Publishing Limited

British Library Cataloguing in Publication Data
Woodiwiss, Anthony
Making human rights work globally
1 Human rights
I Title
323

Library of Congress Cataloguing in Publication Data
Data available

ISBN 1-904385-08-7

The twentieth century ended with a single
surviving model of human progress.

George W Bush, Westpoint, June 2002

...a global unity...remains scarcely accessible.
We lose the particular; we've lost the world.

Michel Serres (1995, p 3)

for aya

Preface

In 1995, Benjamin Barber predicted that human rights would be one of the casualties of the then gestating clash between *McWorld* and *Jihad,* between westernisation and those who oppose it. And so it has turned out, thanks to the equally presumptuous and monistic civilisational faiths of Messrs Bin Laden and Bush, who, driven by these faiths, cannot but judge the rights of individuals to be of secondary importance and therefore derogable more or less at will. Had the West not been so careless of the rights of individuals in the developing world for so long, and had Bin Laden and his Taleban allies not been equally careless of them in their struggle to right this wrong, the current war—whether it is called the War on Terrorism or *Jihad*—would not be taking place and the Universal Declaration of Human Rights would have fulfilled the hope of its authors that it would prevent future wars.

If the Universal Declaration has not been able to inspire states and other actors to prioritise respect for the rights of individuals wherever they may live, it is in part because it is not perceived to be a truly cosmopolitan text but, instead, one of basically Western provenance. This has tended to turn the discourse of human rights into a source of affirmation rather than self-criticism for Western states and an irrelevance to much of the world's population, including the Western poor. Hence the developing world's suspicion of the discourse and, apparently corroboratively, the United States' belief that it need not be judged against international human rights standards. In what follows it will be argued that the developing world's suspicion is in part justified, especially by the systematic privileging of 'justiciable' (immediately enforceable at law) civil and political rights over the supposedly merely 'programmatic' (possibly desirable) economic, social and cultural rights (hereafter economic and social rights) that has marked international human rights discourse as it has developed.

Civil and political rights are hard enough to assert for people in legally sophisticated societies where the notion of the individual is deeply embedded in the culture—I am not at all sure that I have ever asserted my liberties. However, I am very sure and appreciative of the fact that I have, as the saying goes, 'enjoyed' them throughout my life. What has made this enjoyment possible is the additional fact that respect for the same liberties has been built into the routines of British social life by previous generations who created social movements—notably, but not solely, trade unions and political parties—that insisted on the requisite legislation and its enforcement. In this way, then, a set of diffuse liberties that had to be asserted individually was translated into specific, everyday expectations of others or the state that may be usefully referred to as Incidents of liberty' in order to make their filiation explicit. Such expectations thus became enforceable as justiciable claims to, for example, the payment of wages, contract fulfilment, trade union membership, collective bargaining, education, health, and housing, that could be enjoyed. These are the claims that entered international human rights discourse as economic and social rights only to be derogated when, reflecting Cold War divisions, they were assigned programmatic rather than justiciable status in the 1950s, during the negotiations over the formulation of the first two United Nations Covenants: the International Covenant on Civil and Political Rights (ICCPR) and the International Covenant on Economic, Social and Cultural Rights (ICESCR). In what follows, I will argue that the reversal of this derogation is essential if the international human rights regime is to be reformed so that it might at last become an effective means not only of protecting the rights of individuals in non-Western societies, but also of preventing war.

More technically, my argument for reform begins with a positive sociological reading of the conclusions to Wesley Hohfeld's (1919) seminal essay on rights. Subsequent jurisprudence has tended to read Hohfeld negatively as demonstrating incoherences in rights discourse because he pointed out, for example, that liberties were not the same as claims. But sociologically he may be seen as having indicated that liberties and claims are simply different but equally rightful ways of achieving the same or very similar ends with respect to social being. The plausibility and utility of this sociological reading is established below through a comparative account of the development of labour rights across a diverse array of countries—Britain, the United States, France, Sweden, Australia, Japan, Argentina, Brazil, Taiwan, Hong Kong, and Singapore. In the course of this analysis and in view of the obvious salience of Asia to the future of the human rights project—if it fails there, it fails globally—particular attention is paid to developing a response to the issues raised by the proponents of 'Asian values'.

Only in the case of the United States are labour's rights rooted in what Hohfeld termed liberties. In all other cases, often equivalent and sometimes better levels of protection from abuse are achieved through one or other of the alternative juristic mechanisms specified by Hohfeld. Thus only in the United States do civil and political rights provide the key to labour's protection. In all the others economic and social rights fulfil this role. This discovery prompts my principal proposal for the reform of international human rights practice. This is, that the UN should be allowed to sanction not derogations of civil and political rights, but translations of them into economic and social rights, or indeed vice versa, where this is deemed culturally necessary to the achievement of the desired protection. In this way the tension between the two sets of rights that is a product of their Cold War origins could at last be overcome, since their oft asserted 'indivisibility' would have been transformed from a forlorn hope into a facilitative relationship that should also contribute to the transformation of human rights into an instance of a cosmopolitanism truly so called because it is respectful of difference. The book continues by spelling out the practical consequences of this reform proposal for the World Trade Organization's proposed Social Clause and the international acceptability of China's current reforms to its labour rights system. The book ends by thinking about the geopolitical conditions that might allow my reform proposal to be taken up.

In developing this argument I have benefited immensely from the support and help of a large number of institutions and people. I have tried to indicate the specifics of my debts in the main body of the text, but I would like to acknowledge some of them in advance. Thus I would like to thank the Departments of Sociology at City and Hong Kong Universities and the Guangdong Academy of Social Sciences for, in turn, the leave, the visiting fellowship and the permissions and introductions that made the underlying research possible. I would also like to thank the following for permissions to use small and large fragments of earlier versions of parts of what follows: The Asia-Europe Foundation, Cambridge University Press, Sage Publications, *Theory, Culture and Society,* Peter Lang Publishers, and the International Association of Labour History Institutes. Finally, the following individuals deserve special thanks: David Levin for invaluable help in constructing the interview schedule; David Zhao for sharing his deep knowledge of China and superb translating; Beverley Brown for her excellent and very necessary editing; Rod Broadhurst for being a friend in deed; and my partner, Aya Tokita-Woodiwiss, for her patience, support and love.

Anthony Woodiwiss
Chinese University, Hong Kong,
January 2003

I have taken the opportunity to add some further thoughts in the light of recent events in Iraq (p 113).

London,
May 2003

Contents

Introduction
Human rights as means

> The 'human rights box' is a set of historical and social circumstances that enables the human rights framework to gain currency among elites while limiting advances, and even creating setbacks among the general population. Metaphorically, the box contains a universe of options and opportunities for the few while sealing off the vast majority (Bauer, 2000).

The aims of the present study are twofold. First, to explain how the human rights box was so constructed that some in the South now prefer to refer to its contents as 'inhuman rights' (Pereira, 1997). And secondly, to break it open so that human rights discourse may truly become what many have hoped it would be, namely an instrument of protection available to the global majority. Use of the term 'instrument' to refer to human rights may seem surprising and even insufficiently dignified. This is because rights are currently most often spoken of as if they were fundamental ethical principles. They are not. Of course they were inspired by one such principle—in the words of the Universal Declaration, the 'recognition of the inherent dignity...of all members of the human family'—but, as is immediately evident from a consideration of the content of the pertinent texts, they do not themselves restate this principle. Instead, their relationship to this principle is one of means to an end, albeit means that should, I agree, be accorded the same status as principles. However, their elevated honorific status does not change their logical status. It merely reflects the melancholy fact that the end they serve is not an exalted one since it is protective rather than aspirational in nature. As such it testifies to humankind's capacity for evil (cf Badiou, 2001), whether it be the physical torture or the overworking of others, rather than humanity's potential for good. The realisation that human rights are means rather than ends is, as I intend to demonstrate in the body of the text, an intellectually liberatory realisation in that it provides the key with which the human rights box may be sociologically unlocked.

Put in the briefest possible way, the reason why human rights are so often mistaken for ends is because of the wider social context in which they developed. That is, neither the end of protecting human dignity, nor human rights as particular means, were derived from a single set of ethical principles, but from at least two. One was the liberalism that informed the enumeration of civil and political rights, and the other was the socialism which played the same role in relation to economic and social rights. The strongest proponent of the former was the United States, whilst that of the latter was the Soviet Union. Thus in the context of the Cold War, human rights became simply one more arena of super-power conflict. The result was an at least implicit expectation that, if there were ever to be a victor, that power would insist that its protective ethical regime should displace that of its defeated adversary. In the event, some spokespeople for the victorious West have gone much further and claimed that the victory of their side vindicates not simply the protective aspect of their ideology but its aspirational aspect too, with the result that we are now supposedly at the 'end of history' (Fukuyama, 1982).

In the main text I will present much evidence for the operation of this conflictual structural logic with respect to the development of international human rights discourse. However, in fact, and fortunately, the victory of the West over the Soviet Union in the Cold War has not been accompanied by any such ethical triumph, even though it has been accompanied by a good deal of triumphalism. This is because the former Soviet Union was not the only sponsor of the economic and social rights it championed. These rights were, and are, also strongly supported by many of the United States' allies in Western Europe and, more recently if more ambivalently, by many Asian governments. I refer to the Asian support as 'ambivalent' because, in some cases and on some readings, especially when it is justified on the basis of 'Asian values', such support for economic and social rights may represent a stratagem for avoiding governmental obligations in respect of civil and political rights. It is because of this ambivalence, then, and in order to prevent it from becoming a danger, that the present argument hinges on a proposed solution to the problem of securing respect for human rights in familialist societies such as those of Asia.

In any event, economic and social rights are, or may be, gradually being reconfirmed as what they always were despite the obfuscations consequent on the exigencies arising from the Cold War, namely a subset of the practical means available to pursue a protective ethical end that can be very variously specified. Two things make the realisation that human rights are means rather than ends intellectually and, indeed, ethically liberatory when it is developed in a sociological context. First, it provides a way of moving beyond what has become one of the principal obstacles to creative thought in the human rights area, namely the by now very ideological debate between advocates of universalism and those of relativism. Secondly, this possibility arises because of the necessarily concrete way in which rights as means are, and indeed have to be, socially specified. Such concreteness makes any claim to, or insistence upon, their universality in precisely the same form everywhere inherently implausible, let alone more difficult, and therefore less compelling ethically.

Thus human rights as means, even as especially valued means, may be regarded as much more malleable than when they are understood as ends. Indeed, as I intend to argue, they may therefore be treated as, in a limited sense, mutually translatable. I use the qualifier 'limited' in connection with the translatability for which I will argue for two reasons. First, legally, no human right may replace any other, given the indivisibility of the two sets of rights and the presence of articles in the ICCPR and the ICESCR that prohibit the use of any right to justify the violation of any other. Secondly, socially no such replacement has been demanded by any influential state or even body of opinion; that is, even when one looks at the most forceful Southern critiques—notably that produced by certain 'conservative' Asian governments—with only slightly more care than usual, what one discovers is that, although there is a great deal of criticism of Western hypocrisy in the application of human rights standards and a more general suspicion of the West's intentions in applying them, there is no overall intellectual rejection of human rights nor even of civil and political rights (Langlois, 2001). Thus, with respect to civil and political rights, there are no principled objections to the protections provided in relation to the physical integrity of individuals, the legal process, nor even to the right to political participation, and the idea that all such rights should be equally available irrespective of religion or gender. This said, there are amongst some Islamic writers, for example, disagreements concerning the nature of 'cruel and unusual punishments', and resistances to allowing believers the freedom to give up their faith and women to choose their husbands. Rather, the principal concern of Asian governmental critics relates to the freedoms of speech and association that the West, and in particular the United States, tends to see as most fundamental, and which some conservative Americans also see as validating the more diffuse 'market populism' they take to be their nation's legitimating ideology (Frank, 2000). The Asian governmental concern is not so much that these liberties might degenerate into license—although there is an element of this—but that their untrammelled expression might lead to breakdowns in social order and therefore interruptions in the development process. In sum, the replacement of civil and political by economic and social rights is neither possible nor something that has been demanded. However, this need not mean that the rigorous observance of one set of rights could not lead to one or more articles in the other set entering a state of abeyance and thus being subject to reactivation only if such rigorous observance is not maintained.

Although some Western governments, understandably, may have been reacting more to the actual human rights records of some of the Asian governments involved rather than to their philosophical positions, there is nevertheless something surprising and, indeed, hypocritical about some Western expressions of horror at Asian concerns. For Western countries too have not only hesitated in giving full support to the freedoms of speech and association, but have indeed imposed restrictions on them, and not just under the exceptional conditions specified in the ICCPR. Thus, for example, Holocaust denial is prohibited in some Western countries and there are limitations on hate speech and pornography in many others; certain religions do not enjoy the same liberties as others, especially if they have been designated as cults or 'fundamentalist'; and labour's freedom of association has been subject to extensive and widespread limitations. More disturbingly, the British and American governments have also shown themselves willing to compromise even that most basic of civil and political rights represented by the writ of *habeas corpus,* in the context of the current, so-called War on Terrorism (Dworkin, 2002; Talbot, 2002).

There is much more that could be said about each of these sets of limitations—for example, it is very difficult for any Western nation to make claims about its support for, or even enjoyment of, freedom of expression once one thinks in the broader terms represented by the concepts of freedom of information and freedom of communication (Hamelink, 1994; Fisher and Harris, 1983; Mehra, 1986; Rucker, 1968), since both in the West itself and globally the means of information and communication are largely in a few corporate hands. In this text, though, I wish to make my point by restricting myself to some of the issues surrounding labour's freedom of association. Thus the limited translation I will focus on involves the civil and political right to freedom of association, on the one hand, and a range of economic and social rights on the other, since such a translation seems critical with respect to the global acceptability of Asian, and indeed many Southern, social differences.

The need for a sociology of human rights

From a sociologist's point of view, the most obvious evidence of the need for a sociological approach to human rights is that, with the exception of an individually excellent but unconnected series of works by Ted Benton (1993), Bryan Turner (1993), Fred Twine (1994), Boaventura de Sousa Santos (1995), Kevin Bales (1999), and Stan Cohen (2000), there simply is no sociological approach. Thus, even a very recent textbook, such as *International Human Rights in Context: Law, Politics, Morals* (Steiner and Alston, 1996–2001) which, as its title suggests, is committed to the view that human rights can only be properly understood in their wider philosophical, political and social setting, contains only one reference to, and only one extract from, the works of sociologists in its 1,245 pages—Tom Marshall and Steven Lukes. However, sociological silence is not in itself a sufficient justification for sociological talk, especially amongst non-sociologists! It is fortunate therefore that even, at this early stage of development, it is possible to point to a more substantial justification for a sociology of human rights: namely, the possibility that it may immediately make a contribution to the self-evidently social and sociological issues associated with the *global enforceability* of human rights in the very diverse social contexts in which such protection is now possible, as well as necessary.

Beyond the immediate issue of enforceability, there is a space and a need for a more general sociology of human rights. As I envision it, such a sociology would be a very substantial enterprise. It would cover, minimally: the historical study of the development of human rights discourse in both its theoretical and practical, as well as national and global, incarnations; its inclusions and exclusions; the variation in its institutional and social-structural supports and challenges; the unevenness of its effectiveness across the range of rights and in relation to various categories of human beings, as differentiated, for example, by sex, gender, 'race', ethnicity, religion, and sexual orientation; the strengths and weaknesses of different mechanisms of enforcement and the difficulties of assessing their effectiveness; and, finally, its possible futures. Clearly, the present study does not, and indeed could not, claim to be anything other than a very partial realisation of this vision. At its core is a sustained case study of the human rights pertaining to labour that takes the form of a cross-section through many of the issues just listed.

Although I will derive some general lessons from this exercise, realisation of the larger vision will clearly require the completion of many such cross-sections relating to different spheres of social relations. This said, and despite the current unfashionableness of labour rights on the Left and their anathematisation on the American Right (Gould, 2000), I am unapologetic about such a focus. A focus on labour rights suits my technical purpose in that they are both civil and political, and economic and social, and so readily lend themselves to an investigation of the possibility of mutual translation. Also, labour rights are the rights most often and universally violated, as is suggested by the fact that, according to the International Labour Organization (ILO), more than two million people die each year from work-related injuries or illnesses, which is three times the number of people who die in wars. Moreover, labour disputes provide the occasion for many violations of other civil and political rights. Finally, despite the complacency of some of the beneficiaries of earlier struggles (see below, p 29), the systematic violation of labour rights in many societies today has resulted in a terrifying global revival of the slavery prohibited by Article 8 of the ICCPR which means that, on a conservative estimate, some 27 million people worldwide—including thousands in Western Europe and the United States—are currently enslaved (Bales, 1999, pp 3, 8–9). This is because what Kevin Bales has called the 'new slavery' no longer depends on the ownership of persons, but on an oppressive level of control over them made possible by the absence of labour law or the weakness of its enforcement; that is, when, as in the case of many illegal migrants in the West, a person cannot freely choose his or her work, insist on certain minimum conditions relating to wage levels, health and safety, hours of work, rest periods and holidays, join a trade union, or participate in social insurance schemes, such a person becomes a slave since there is no limit on what he or she can be required to do and no guarantee of payment (see also Mehmet *et al*, 1999).

As against what many sociologists have argued in the past (Abel, 1982; de Sousa Santos, 1995, for example), my main purpose in closely examining this aspect of law will not be to find surrogates for legal institutions, although there are circumstances in which such surrogates have an important role to play, as in the case of truth commissions (Hayner, 2001; Wilson, 2000). Rather, my aim is to consider how, by translating socially non-pertinent legal statuses and entitlements into socially pertinent ones, legal discourse itself may be made both more effective and less culturally intrusive or destructive. In this regard, the recent development and deployment by the European Court of Human

Rights of the doctrines known as the 'margin of appreciation' (member states should have some discretion as to how they fulfil their obligations) and the 'effectiveness principle' (member states should ensure that their citizens may practically exercise their rights) seem most encouraging. This is because these doctrines allow the blurring of the distinction between civil and political and economic and social rights, and suggest that the translations I have in mind could be seen as acceptable when judged against the principles of international human rights law. Moreover, they have already been used in labour cases (Merrils, 1988, Chapters 5 and 6, and pp 222–23; Yourow, 1995).

Thus when one argues that rights should be understood as means rather than ends, and therefore to a limited degree as mutually translatable, it becomes clear that the purpose of human rights is not to insist on the organisation or re-organisation of social life around one or other set of aspirational principles. Rather, their purpose is to ensure the maintenance of certain very basic conditions of human being (freedom from torture, hunger, or overwork, for example) and pertinent forms of action (freedoms of speech, association, and collective bargaining, for example) in very different social contexts. And what this means in turn is both that human rights discourse may be freed from the burden of specifying the good for the world and, as important, that the pursuit and definition of the good may continue as an open-ended and universal activity rather than being monopolised by those countries and ideologies that are presently powerful—for surely humanity is still capable of aspiring to more than freedom from mutual abuse, and in many different ways? Thus I do not fully agree with those who argue for bringing politics and political theory back into human rights discourse (Campbell *et al*, 2001; Douzinas, 2000; Langlois, 2001)—politics may be unavoidable, but political theory should be reserved for imagining the good rather than risking the complication and delay of the struggle against a set of evils that are understood all too well.

An outline of the argument

I will begin this outline with a very brief overview of the book before moving on to provide a longer, more analytical account of the argument. Chapter 1 sets out the theoretical framework that informs the remainder of the text. In Chapter 2 this framework is deployed to produce a schematic sociological account of the rise of international human rights discourse as a global phenomenon. Chapters 3 and 4 build upon the arguments developed in the preceding chapters and my earlier work in the area of labour rights (Woodiwiss, 1990b, 1992, 1998). The following two chapters extend the same mode of analysis to what are, for me, new objects of interest—specifically, the international and Chinese systems of labour rights—in order to demonstrate the practical utility of the mode of analysis.

To elaborate on this overview, two points particularly recommend a focus on labour rights. First, such a focus takes us to the heart of the presently pressing question of the relative status of, and the relationship between, civil and political and economic and social rights. As very quickly becomes clear in any encounter with the human rights literature or politics, this is a very fraught and contextually sensitive issue which divides North and South as well as East and West. Moreover, this very difficulty makes it a good point of entry for a sociologist, since none of the existing human rights disciplines (law, philosophy, ethics, political science, and anthropology) has got very far with it. In my view, the reason for this failure has been the lure of the 'great debate' about whether rights are universal or culturally relative, contributions to which have too often given credence to the pernicious doctrine of the 'clash of civilisations' (for some exceptions, see An-Na'im, 1990; Bauer and Bell, 1999; Wilson, 1996). Instead, given the actually minimal character of the differences involved (see above, p 3), my view is that one should simply accept these differences and seek ways of articulating them with one another within a transnational context. Secondly, a focus on labour rights also takes us to the heart of the linked and equally pressing, but more practical, political question of how China should be understood and responded to within the context of the current global human rights regime, given its difficulties with the ideas underpinning civil and political rights.

Within these contexts, then, Chapter 2 locates one source of the problems currently faced by the discourse of international human rights, as it has developed within the UN, in the absence from the discourse of any acknowledgment of the pertinence of the social-structural differences exhibited by its member states, save for their level of economic development. It further argues that the problems, again unacknowledged, that this absence creates have been compounded by three factors. First, the rise of the doctrine of justiciability (the doctrine that the only 'real' rights are those that are instantly enforceable by courts) which presently privileges civil and political over economic and social rights. Secondly, contrary to the implications of the right to self-determination, the artificial narrowing of what might be termed 'allowable' social-structural differences to economic ones, which in turn rests on the developed/undeveloped distinction, and implies an unacknowledged and largely Ameri-centric evolutionism in which the present nature of the 'modern', American-led West defines the best or even the only possible future for the less developed world. Thirdly, and relatedly, there is a serious failing—maybe wilful, maybe not—on the part of the representatives of some Western states to understand the highly restricted nature of the entitlements that economic and social rights represent—not cake every day for all but a democratically and locally defined minimal share of whatever cake is going.

It is surely time that the taint of 'Stalinism' was finally removed from the concept of economic and social rights. Such rights are far more obviously derived from the broad, Western European traditions of Christian and Social Democracy than from the ideology of the Stalinist, or even post-Stalinist, Soviet Union, regardless of the strong support they had from that quarter. As elements of these non-communist traditions, and indeed of the social structures in which they are embedded, economic and social rights have long had to co-exist, as they do in the Universal Declaration of Human Rights, with a right to private property which sets rather stringent limits to any redistributive implications they may have. As one of the most articulate and clear-headed spokesmen for these non-communist traditions, Marshall (1994), pointed out many years ago, economic and social rights in both theory and practice are essentially culturally determined statuses and they therefore seek only to ensure equal respect for all citizens in the sense of an equal opportunity to compete on the basis of a locally agreed minimum for a civilised life. Thus, fortunately or unfortunately, far from being the harbingers of a material equality that some appear to fear, such rights in fact, to use Marshall's words, 'operate as…instrument[s] of stratification'. That is, they do not dissolve the inequalities intrinsic to capitalist societies but simply change the nature of the competition for whatever rewards it offers—whatever the baseline, higher rewards are always available.

Chapter 2 approaches its end by spelling out the negative consequences of these narrow and misunderstood conceptions for the poorer peoples of less developed societies—irrespective of the fact that a country's poverty need be no bar to the introduction of justiciable economic and social rights and regardless of the ready local cultural acceptability of such rights, the world's poorest people are denied access to the law because of an entirely unwarranted and, I would say, mean-spirited fear of what the law could do for them. The chapter concludes by outlining two steps that might be taken to ameliorate the situation. The first is the suggestion, justified in Chapters 3 and 4, that there is a way in which the UN could begin to take economic and social rights as well as social-structural differences seriously, and that is to be willing to engage in a process of sociologically informed conceptual translation between the ICCPR and the ICESCR. This mode of translation is made possible by, on the one hand, the discovery of the template for a non-liberal human rights regime that is latent within contemporary familialist discourses of rule and, on the other, the re-invigoration of the doctrine of the indivisibility of the two sets of rights. The non-liberal human rights regime I have in mind is that which I term 'enforceable benevolence' and is made possible by the realisation that there is no necessary antipathy between familialism and human rights (see below, pp 50–55), once the latter's instrumental and narrowly protective character is recognised. This in turn depends upon the realisation that it is both more useful, and indeed intellectually more defensible, to distinguish between different kinds of rights on the basis of how they achieve their effects, whether (drawing upon Hohfeld) as claims or liberties, for example, rather than on the basis of their substantive character as either civil and political or economic and social. The doctrine of indivisibility is what Ann Kent (1993) summarises so well when, paraphrasing Henry Shue (1980), she talks of civil and political rights resting on a basic right 'to life' whilst economic and social rights rest on an equivalent right 'to live'. In my view, the translation capability made available by the combination of these two sets of ideas—by the recognition that the same substantive right may be protected in different ways—is what at last allows the current international bill of rights not only to be made pertinent to local conditions, but also both to remain justiciable and retain its claim to universality. The second step is the suggestion, developed in Chapter 5, that the inclusion of a Social Clause, re-written to make it globally more effective than the current draft, in the protocols of the World Trade Organization (WTO) is necessary if at least some economic and social rights are at last to be enforced at the global level.

Chapter 6 exemplifies the effects of taking these two steps by deploying the ideas that lie behind them in the course of an analysis of current conditions and possibilities in the critical case of Southern China. The Conclusion does two things. First, it suggests how the argument for the intertranslatability of the ICCPR and the ICESCR in the labour sphere might be extended to other spheres. Secondly, it discusses the problems and possibilities created for my proposal by the fact that the United States is both the sole remaining superpower and the most significant non-ratifier of the ICESCR.

Finally, in order to try to prevent a likely misunderstanding, I would like to end this introduction by making it clear that what follows is most definitely not an argument for social and economic over civil and political rights, but simply one that seeks to make use of the established legal and geopolitical doctrine—though it is too often honoured only in the breach—as to the equality and indivisibility of the two sets of rights. Whilst the two sets of rights may never be wholly substituted for each other because of the irreducible and valued differences in their underlying ethics, some at least of the component rights in each set may sometimes be re-written in terms of one another for the sake of assuring effective protection in very diverse social circumstances. Thus, although I will focus on contemporary circumstances in which I believe that the dignity of individuals can be more effectively protected when liberties are translated into claims on employers and/or states, whether civil and political or economic and social, I do not rule out the reverse mode of translation (that is, translating claims into liberties). Moreover, the latter strategy might be especially appropriate where there are serious doubts about a state's ability to fulfil any claims it might be expected to meet, whether because it lacked the institutional capacity, as in Robert Jackson's (1990) 'quasi-states', or the necessary integrity, as in Peter Evans' (1995) 'predatory states'.

A world divided by huge political and economic inequalities (Bradshaw and Wallace, 1996) is a world where trust between nations is in very short supply and enmity may easily arise. Here one may reasonably call upon sociology's claimed capacity to be a conduit for cultural sophistication. Sociological investigations, techniques of argument and modes of assessment promise to provide a new type of confidence-building measure. The next time a state, as they often do, invokes social reasons for entering a 'reservation' with respect to a particular human rights treaty, or argues that it should benefit from a 'margin of appreciation' in relation to a supposedly faulty piece of legislation or an alleged violation, the other states parties should find here a resource that will enable them to distinguish between arguments made in good, as opposed to bad, sociological faith.

Chapter 1
Theorising a global social fact

In its broadest, generic sense the discourse of human rights has a very long history, in that many very diverse societies and civilisations have recognised the extreme vulnerability of individual human beings and sought ways in which they might be protected from some of the more oppressive possibilities that therefore arise (Ishay, 1997; Lauren, 1998, Chapter 1). For this reason the possible scope of a sociology of human rights is also very broad. The focus of the present text, however, is rather narrow in that, despite often using the terms 'human rights' and 'international human rights' interchangeably, my focus will be more precisely on the latter rather than the former. This is because my central object of concern is that variety of human rights discourse that has become a component of the global social order as it has emerged since the ending of World War II. Certainly I will show that this discourse displays an excessive dependence upon ideas and techniques of what, for simplicity's sake, I will term 'Western' provenance, but I will not argue that the discourse should be displaced from its present pre-eminence for that reason. Instead, I will argue not only that it *should* be made more truly cosmopolitan in its constitutive ideas, but also that it *can* be so transformed. For these reasons, whilst what follows recognises, and indeed values, the diversity of local human rights discourses, it is not concerned to explain this diversity, important though such work would be, but instead with the more immediate problems of why this diversity is not fully reflected in the international discourse, and how this problem might be overcome.

Although the present prominence of international human rights discourse is the result of the actions of huge numbers of individuals and organisations from all parts of the globe, it also exceeds what would be possible through the sheer aggregation of these efforts. That is, as an aspect of globalisation it is the result of not only a visible synergy of all these actions, as exemplified by the numerous meetings and conferences that mark the history of its emergence, but also of an invisible and arguably even more effective synergy of what Emile Durkheim (1895) termed *sui generis* social facts; and as a synergy, it is an instance of what one of his followers, Marcel Mauss (1924), termed a 'total social fact'. In other words, human rights discourse is an aspect of a complex social entity that is greater than the sum of its parts, and so not only subject to a distinctive dynamic but capable of producing autonomous effects (Woodiwiss, 1998, pp 22–24). More concretely, what this means is that some at least of the power invested in human rights discourse by individuals, governments and other social actors as it has developed is unreturnable. It is therefore available to discipline these same actors not only in the controllable formal manner instanced by UN processes, but also in more socially diffuse and uncontrollable ways—exemplified by the often highly effective charges of hypocrisy levelled at the United States by some Muslim human rights activists as well as states.

The story of the visible synergy that produced and maintains human rights discourse has been told very well many times already, notably by Antonio Cassese (1990), Paul Gordon Lauren (1998) and, refreshingly critically, Kirsten Sellars (2002), but that of the invisible synergy that sociologists are interested in exists only in the form of a very brief, general and, as he would readily admit, incomplete sketch by Roland Robertson (see below, pp 22–23), which was anyway written for another purpose. This imbalance between the level of development of the two stories is a problem for at least two reasons. First, it makes it appear that self-conscious human and organisational effort has been a far more important determinant of the discourse's rise to prominence than global social-structural developments (Woodiwiss, 2001 a, conc)—a proposition which, as a particular kind of sociologist, I have to say is very doubtful. Secondly, if the social-structural causes of the discourse's rise and disciplinary effectiveness are unknown, then accurately diagnosing the sources of any difficulties it faces is impossible and so, therefore, is effective action to resolve them.

Overcoming the reticence of sociology

Until recently, a major reason for the absence of the sociological part of the story has been a combination of the discipline's theoretical underdevelopment and a simple lack of interest. These at least are the problems that I will address in this chapter by outlining a theoretical framework for the production of a sociology of, and approach to, human rights. The reasons why sociology has been so slow to interest itself in human rights are threefold, and to list them is instructive because it will tell us much about the changes the discipline has had to undergo in order that it might now be able to make its contribution to the understanding of human rights.

Aside from a suspicion of the idea of natural rights inherited from Bentham and Marx, the most fundamental reason for the discipline's reticence concerning human rights has been its largely unconscious identification of society with the nation state (Mann, 1986, Chapter 1). This has meant that until recently it has lacked the theoretical means necessary to grasp the nature of, let alone investigate, human rights as a global phenomenon. By the same token, however, sociology's concern with the nation state should also mean that it is very well placed to provide an understanding of the local conditions that either favour or undermine the possibility of respect for human rights. This is despite two other aspects of its recent past which have meant that for the last 20 years many sociologists have not been able to take either social structure or rights very seriously. Thus the second of the reasons for sociology's reticence was, compared to other academic disciplines, the belated eruption within it of a Postmodernism of a basically literary provenance which called into question the reality of both social structure and rights. The result has been that the attention of many theoretically talented sociologists has been redirected to issues of individual and collective identities which are seen as largely willed constructs constituted within social-structural and legal conditions, but, strangely, not constrained by them, since such conditions are regarded, practically if not theoretically, as themselves mere representations whose effects, therefore, can be either chosen or disregarded (see Gergen, 1991; Hall and Du Gay, 1996; Jenkins, 1996; and, for a critique, Craib, 1998). A third and related reason for the reticence with respect to human rights was a more specific lack of interest within the most pertinent sub-discipline, the Sociology of Law. Here interest was discouraged both by a politically determined obsession with the criminal law, reflected in the distribution of research funding, and by local variants of the first two reasons. As a result, municipal law rather than international law is still the focus of the Sociology of Law. In addition, the rise of the Critical Legal Studies Movement facilitated the entry of Postmodernism into the area with what were initially very damaging consequences for work on rights, since, in an overreaction to what Michael Ignatieff (2001, pp 82ff) has justifiably termed 'human rights idolatry', they tended to be seen as rather noxious phantasms (Douzinas, 2000; Gaete, 1993).

All that said, what a recovering sociology immediately has to offer the international human rights project is an understanding of both its genesis and the global and local difficulties that it faces with respect to enforcement. This is because sociology is now characterised by a new focus on the global, it exhibits a revived interest in social structure and an improved understanding of the nature of the law and rights, and it possesses a means of bringing all of this to bear on the issues of enforceability and enforcement. As I have argued elsewhere in the course of critical discussions of the globalisation literature (Woodiwiss, 1998, Chapter 1; Woodiwiss, 2001a, conc), we can now grasp the following analytically significant points: (1) globalisation as a 'total social fact' is not simply a product and an instantiation of transnational political, economic and cultural developments, but also of distinguishable international structures and flows and *always* the reciprocal interactions of transnational and international forces with localities—that is, globalisation makes the whole world *'active'*, not just its Western parts; (2) not only are national borders porous because of the multiple dimensions of the transnational/international/local interface, but also all nation states have become ever more hybridised and for the same reasons—that is, globalisation does not mean westernisation (contra Giddens, 1990); (3) globalisation is only one of the possible outcomes of transnational/international/local interactions—that is, globalisation is not inevitable. In sum, and as Robertson (1990) above all has made clear, the present prominence of human rights discourse is both a product of the myriad other processes driving globalisation, and a potential victim if they go into reverse.

In the current context, the most immediately pertinent consequence of accepting these three propositions, and the multi-dimensional conception of globalisation to which they lead (Woodiwiss, 2001a), is the rejection of Samuel Huntington's 'clash of civilisations' thesis. For Huntington, the world is divided into eight distinct civilisational blocs, nine if Africa is considered a civilisation! Formally, each bloc is to be accorded the same respect and the same right to exist, except that only one, 'Western Civilisation', is explicitly defined in coherent and positive terms whilst all the others are defined fragmentarily and negatively. The problem is not only that this mode of presentation suggests bias by an unconscious Ameri-centrism that does not acknowledge Europe's difference, but also that it leads to an exaggerated and a mistaken understanding of the nature of Western distinctiveness—without going into it, much of what he claims to be distinctive about the West may be found in China's past and present, for example. That is, and using his terminology, had Huntington been less blinded by his own civilisation's manifest power and more attentive to the latent power granted to the other civilisations by the integrative forces intrinsic to globalisation, he might have been more attentive to the particularity of the others. In so doing, he would have seen that in today's porous and socially hybridised world, the differences involved are a lot more subtle than he supposes. Moreover, thanks to various colonialisms, one of the main reasons for the commonality he denies is the presence of a set of elements that were indeed initially characteristic of, as well as unique to, the whole West, and whose existence he steadfastly ignores—namely the economic, political and cultural prerequisites for a capitalist economy in the form of commodity markets (including one for labour) and appropriate forms of the state and law. Thus, even though human rights, as both a facilitator and an antidote to the same capitalism, may also have been initially unique to the West, there is nothing intrinsically alien about human rights in any part of the world now, and therefore no necessary reason why they should represent either an instance, or an occasion, of any 'clash of civilisations'—even if there may be a host of other reasons for doubting the universality of particular understandings of their content and policy implications.

Theory and the recognition of social difference

Concerning the law and rights, and to repeat more or less verbatim some of what I have written elsewhere (Woodiwiss, 1990b, Chapter 5; 1998, Chapter 1), the foundational and constitutive role of the methodological requirement for 'consistency' on the part of judges and jurists is what gives legal discourse its possibility of autonomy. However, 'consistency' is never either a sufficient or a self-subsisting sign in legal, or in any other form of, discourse. Legal consistency must, therefore, always be a means of ensuring that a substantive principle applies equally to all, to those that enunciate the law as well as to those to whom it is perhaps more directly addressed. It therefore must always be articulated with some such substantive principle—for example, 'liberty', 'equality' or 'familialism' in their multiple specifications and combinations—before it can have an effect. In sum, contrary to Western prejudice, the rule of law is not to be identified with a particular political philosophy—liberalism, but rather with a social-structural effect, namely the reduction of arbitrariness (Unger, 1976; Woodiwiss, 1990b, Part III). Thus, whether or not any substantive, as opposed to merely formal, consistency and judicial autonomy exists, and so how the law can operate as a defence of human rights, must vary—and vary quite markedly—according to the more general social-structural background with which it is necessarily imbricated. This, then, is why, first, law must be congruent with—and in this sense embedded within—the wider discourses, structures and practices of a society if it is to be enforceable, as well as why, secondly, judicial particularism and/or inactivity, rather than lack of concern for liberty, should be taken as the principal sign that the rule of law may be under threat.

This de-historicised way of thinking about law opens possibilities for developing a strategy for embedding respect for human rights within the social structures of non-liberalistic societies. In order to take full advantage of these possibilities, three additional theoretical moves are necessary. The first is to reject the humanist, essentialist and Euro-centric—that is, the commonsensically liberal—conception of human rights as the natural rights of individuals, and to replace it with a decidedly more mundane, but theoretically liberating, legal positivist conception of rights as simply discursive entities which serve 'certain socially determined policy objectives and interests' (Hirst, 1979, p 104). The second and related move is to recognise that to view rights as discursive entities immediately raises questions as to whether and how rights are socially 'connected' with the agents, human or otherwise, that are their supposed bearers.

The third theoretical move is to reject the conventional differentiation of positive and negative rights which underpins all the UN's central texts and which, in the Anglo-American world at least, continues to evoke the liberalistic preference for the latter that was so famously expressed by Sir Isaiah Berlin (1969, Chapter 3), and has recently been very elegantly restated by Michael Ignatieff (2001). Here what I have in mind is that one should instead follow Carl Wellman's (1989) lead and extend to human rights Wesley Hohfeld's anti-naturalistic and pluralistic conception of 'jural' or legal relations, but with this difference: that the term 'right' be used to refer to jural relations as a whole rather than to one particular type of such relation (see also Halpin, 1997, Chapter 2). Thus rights may be understood as discursively defined clusters of: 'liberties' to perform certain actions; 'claims' or expectations vis à vis specified others; 'powers' that allow legal subjects to assume certain specified roles and change certain social relations; and 'immunities' against prosecution and/or civil suit when pursuing ends that are otherwise defined as illegal.

What I wish to suggest, then, is that human rights may be effective policy instruments, despite their uneven development along one or more of Hohfeld's dimensions and their lack of effectiveness with respect to the less developed of these dimensions. That is, given the mutually implicatory character of the different forms of rights and the similarity of their social consequences, and although 'liberties', etc, are ultimately irreducible to one another, the more, so to speak, there is of one, the less need there is for the others. To elaborate, if 'liberties' are clearly and broadly defined, there is less need for their implications in terms of 'claims' or whatever to be spelt out, since the existence of the latter are socially implied, albeit as available as a last resort in order to enable people to exercise their liberties—for example, even the United States has some sort of social safety net. Likewise, if 'claims', for example, are clearly and broadly defined, there is no need for their implications in terms of 'liberties' or whatever to be spelt out, since acceptance of the existence of 'claims' against one, or indeed the state, socially implies acceptance of another's 'liberty' to require their satisfaction, albeit again as a last resort, as seems to be the case in Japan. The social behaviours directly protected by 'claims' will not necessarily be the same as those protected as 'liberties'—for example, attending a mediatory hearing rather than striking—but the effect of protection should nevertheless be a similarly balancing one as regards the asymmetrical social relations within which concerns as to respect for human rights arise. This is because the protection of 'claims' behaviours represents a limitation on the freedom of the more powerful by imposing a duty or obligation on them; a mode of limitation that may be much more strongly supported and, indeed, more safely asserted, given particular cultural and social-structural circumstances, than might be the case where what is at stake is in the first instance one of the less powerful's 'liberties'.

Because it opens the way for the development of a non-Ameri-centric concept of human rights, this is an argument that has both sociological and political significance. I will reserve a discussion of its political significance to later chapters. Sociologically, it specifies, far more concretely than has hitherto been the case, what is involved in the task of investigating the social embeddedness of human rights. That is, the discursive gulf between the language of the law and that of sociology appears to be far less glaring than otherwise seems to be the case. In other words, whereas there has generally been something about the language of rights that social scientists baulk at—hence Jeremy Bentham's reference to natural rights as 'nonsense on stilts' and the Marxist talk of them as 'mystifications' and products of 'commodity fetishism'—there is much less of a problem when the Hohfeldian language is used. Indeed, it seems to me to be relatively easy to see how such concepts as capitalism and class, and their specification in terms of possession and separation from the means of production, may be brought to bear on such questions as to whether or not particular individuals possess 'liberties' to perform certain actions or can enforce their 'claims' on others (and vice versa, of course). This is because, for example, limitations on possession/separation imply restrictions on liberties' and/or 'claims', whilst enhanced liberties' and/or 'claims' imply reduced separation and enhanced possession.

What all of this means, then, for the capitalist employment relation within which the labour rights of concern in the present text have their primary effects, is that one can see very clearly how labour law is both affected in its content and enforcement *by* class balances, and is also constitutive of the same balances. Here I will speak only of the constitutive role of law, since this enables one to summarise the possible effects on class balances of the law's content. In sum, when one brings the Marxist and Hohfeldian concepts together one may both grasp something of the complexity of the relationship between the law and class relations and explain how it is that labour law represents an index of class balances:

(a) The law may alter the balance with respect to the economic *possession* of the means of production to labour's advantage by granting certain 'liberties' to bargain over the terms of employment and/or by inscribing certain 'claims' within the conditions governing the hiring of labour, and therefore the validity of the employment contract. These are generally referred to as 'labour standards', and include rules governing the payment of wages, rest periods, and holidays. However, they also include such aspects of collective labour law as those pertaining to the permissability or otherwise of the closed shop. The inscription of such 'liberties' and/or 'claims' may or may not be accompanied by the granting to labour of participative 'powers' of one kind or another with respect to the setting of such standards.

(b) The law may alter the balance with respect to political or disciplinary *control* of the means of production to labour's advantage in three ways: first, by granting certain 'liberties' to bargain over the conditions of employment and/or by inscribing certain 'claims' within the employment contract in the form of those aspects of 'labour standards' that refer to workplace rules; secondly, by limiting the contract's purview through specifying certain additional 'liberties' which may allow its temporary suspension for bargaining purposes; thirdly, by specifying in either workplace rules and/or the employment contract certain 'claims' that allow for the exercise of 'powers' of one kind or another which allow varying degrees of co-determination as well as the adjudication of disputes by tripartite tribunals or mutually agreed third parties.

(c) The law may alter the balance with respect to *title* to the means of production to labour's advantage by granting certain liberties to bargain over ownership and/or by inscribing various 'claims' within property, company and taxation law in order to achieve such as profit-sharing, employee share-ownership, nationalisation, and/or to distribute social benefits of one kind or another. Again, the inscription of such claims may or may not be accompanied by the granting of certain participative 'powers' to labour at the enterprise and/or national levels.[1]

All that said, a problem nevertheless arises when one attempts the transfer of insights generated within the sociology of law to the realm of human rights. This problem is municipal or national law's assumption of, in broad terms, a socially homogenous jurisdiction. As each of the classical sociological writers—Marx, Weber and Durkheim—recognised in their own ways, law is a very important but nevertheless, in a certain sense, 'secondary force in human affairs' (Kahn-Freund, 1977) in that it can only really work when it mobilises pre-existing forces within social structures, as is very clearly illustrated even with regard to one of the judiciary's greatest triumphs, namely the American Supreme Court's decision in *Brown v Board of Education* (1954) (347 US 483) which was only enforced for as long as it was because of the Civil Rights Movement and subsequent forms of African-American political mobilisation. Thus in the last analysis it is not the existence of police forces, inspectorates, or even independent judiciaries *per se* that assures that the law will be obeyed, but rather the degree to which any law is embedded in, or congruent with, the sets of social relations that it is required to regulate—hence, negatively, the phenomenon of desuetude or dead law, the difficulties of enforcing so-called 'Vice laws' (Woodiwiss, M, 2001b) and the eventual fate of many laws that are considered to be unjust by politically influential groups. In a sociological sense, then, effective law is necessarily conservative. That is, the law can only do what the remainder of the social structure allows it to do, including contributing to social change, if there are supportive social-structural dynamics, and cannot change social relations on its own. Hence it is the hopelessness of police action that kills old laws, the corruption of the police and politicians that allows laws against 'Vice' to survive, and it is only very occasionally that a judge sounds the tocsin of revolt. In sum, a socially incongruent law makes the task of those who are required to enforce it impossible.

The generally well-grounded, and indeed socially determined, assumption of jurisdictional homogeneity is even more of a problem as regards human rights law than it is with respect to other areas of international law, save perhaps for international family law. This is because much of international private law relates to a transnationally homogenous jurisdiction, namely that defined by capitalist enterprise and exchange, whereas human rights law, like international family law, relates to a much more heterogeneous set of social relations. And this is both because of and despite globalisation. The argument to be put forward here may, therefore, be restated and summarised as follows. Like international family law today (van Beuren, 1995, Chapter 3), even colonial legal systems most often recognised that the cultural particularity of family forms justified the maintenance of local family law whilst the remainder of legal life was westernised. Why, then, should we not acknowledge the cultural particularity of personhood, and therefore that there may be social particularities additional to forms of kinship, such as those I will suggest as pertinent to labour rights, that ought to be acknowledged if respect for that personhood is to be enforceable? This, then, is ultimately why I will argue that socio-legal translation should be a part of human rights work.

In order that these new conceptualisations may be combined and made pertinent to international human rights discourse and the question of its enforceability in very diverse social circumstances, they need to be inserted into a broader analytical construct that accounts for the discourse's development and power effects as a total social fact. Fortunately, such a construct is available in the form of Michel Foucault's concepts of the 'discursive formation' and its 'rules of formation' (on the compatibility of Durkheimian and Foucaultian approaches, see Woodiwiss, 2001a). The questions that Foucault addresses with these concepts are: (1) How do discourses develop? (2) How do they come to be taken as comprising authoritative, and therefore to some degree socially determinant, statements about the nature of the world?

His answer to these questions is that discourses develop and gain their determinative power as a consequence of the largely unwilled interaction between four elements: 'objects' (the things they are about); 'modes of enunciation' (the ways these things are spoken of); 'concepts' (the intellectual constructs that are used to speak about them); and 'strategies' (the ways in which these constructs are combined or thematised). What determines the nature and power effects of the interactions between these elements are their respective rules or, better, the social entities and processes that continuously determine their formation and re-formation.

In the case of objects these entities and processes, partially translated from Foucault's rather fearsome terminology, comprise: (1) the institutional sites wherein the 'objects' of interest are problematised and so become socially visible—for example, the Catholic confessional in the case of psychiatry, the marketplace in the case of economics, and the 'court' in the case of law; (2) the appearance or presence of 'authorities of delimitation'—experts and latterly professionals of all kinds—who possess the power to decide what is or is not an instance of the object of interest; and (3) the production or presence of a 'grid of specification' produced by these experts which delimits the object of interest and distinguishes it from other objects—examples include general concepts such as the 'body', the 'economy', the 'polity', 'society', the law', and 'human rights'. Concerning 'enunciative modalities', or ways of making statements, the entities and processes are: (1) the credentials of the qualified speakers; (2) the institutional sites from whence they speak; and (3) the modes of 'interrogation' they engage in (listening, questioning, or looking, for example). With respect to 'concepts', the entities and processes are: (1) their order and forms of succession or emergence and development; (2) their fields and forms of coexistence, or the general methodologies that are used to determine their legitimacy as instances of knowledge; and (3) the 'procedures for intervention', or the ways of working within the conceptual field as exemplified by 're-writing', 'transcribing', and 'translating'. Finally, the entities and processes with regard to 'strategies' are: (1) the identities, similarities, differences, and combinations of such strategies; (2) the identification of thematic authorities, whether these are located within the field of discourse involved or external to it and are therefore authorities by analogy; and (3) the identification of 'the *function* that the discourse under study must carry out *in a field of non-discursive practices*' (Foucault, 1972, p 68, emphasis in original) such as the economic and political realms, and '*possible positions of desire in relation to discourse*' (emphasis in original).

What, in sum, Foucault has provided us with is a means for thinking about and tracking the highly complex concatenations that produce such 'total social facts' as international human rights discourse. Moreover, he has also provided us with a guide as to how intellectuals, including sociologists, might most effectively intervene in this concatenation; that is, not so much by attending to the 'objects' of discourse, since they develop in the ways they do for reasons that are largely beyond human, let alone intellectual, control, but rather by attending to the other three components of discursive formations.

One result of the preliminary application of this analytic carried out in what follows is the establishment of the point that, for good as well as for ill, human rights talk has become ever more clearly an instance of legal discourse. Although one might regret this for substantive practical reasons to do with the limitations it might impose with respect to modes of redressing grievances, it greatly simplifies things analytically since the social nature of the law as such is already well-understood, even if the same cannot be said for global law. Moreover, some reflection on the analytical problem represented by human rights as a global legal phenomenon promises to provide a means by which some of the other problems faced by those concerned with the enforcement of human rights might be overcome.

Notes

1 I owe the tripartite 'sociological' conception of the property relation as consisting of distinguishable relations of possession, control and title to the work of Kelvin Jones (1982, pp 76ff).

As I read Jones, by 'possession' he means the narrowly economic capacity to use or operate the production process at all. By 'control', he means the political ability or power to determine the detailed deployment of means of production in the production process. Finally, what he means by 'title' refers to the cultural or significatory basis upon which claims to any surplus may be made, and so it is not restricted to:

> ...the formal legal right to a claim upon a company or an estate but depends upon the sorts of calculations which govern the circulation of legal titles...title involves the sort of calculations and conditions that govern the more general provision of finance, the socialisation of debt, the exchange of guarantees and the constitutional position of shareholders Jones, 1982, pp 77–78).

In addition, and insightfully, Jones also points out that whereas within small and medium size enterprises the possessory relation is critical, within large corporate enterprises the control relation is critical. Thus, as I have explained elsewhere (Woodiwiss, 1990b, p 272), where labour law systems do not include provisions relating to co-determination and/or title-sharing (for example, the Swedish Wage Earner Funds), which means in most of the world outside of Western Europe, their pertinence is largely confined to a set of relations (possessory) that are of decreasing significance as loci of power within contemporary economies. Consequently, one may argue that the legal position of trade unions has been weakened throughout much of the world as much by the increasing irrelevance of extant labour law as by restrictive 'reforms'.

Chapter 2
International human rights and the silence concerning social difference

For some scholars, the values inscribed within the UN's human rights texts represent an achieved instance of Immanuel Kant's 'cosmopolis'. Would that they did. One of the leading proponents of the cosmopolitan view, David Beetham (1998; see also Marks, 2000, pp 106 ff), acknowledges, however, that problems remain in the areas of implementation and enforcement. I agree, but in what follows I will argue that these problems have roots that reach deep into the innermost structures of the regime itself, and therefore require attention before one can more confidently speak of human rights as a cosmopolitan artefact.

The Western, and in many ways specifically English, origins of the civil and political components of human rights discourse are well-known, as indeed are the equally Western origins of Marx's critique of them in the name of economic and social needs. The trouble is that, despite this knowledge, many participants in the human rights project fail to appreciate not only the continuing salience of these origins, but, perhaps more importantly, the ways in which this salience has been reinvigorated by the continuous reinvention of these Western divisions within the international human rights regime as it has developed since the 1940s.

To my mind, this failure has created at least two interlinked difficulties which currently threaten to derail the project. The first, and more general, difficulty arises because our knowledge of the specific social genealogy of rights discourse is too seldom used as a resource for interrogating the present international discourse. That is, we too seldom compare national rights discourses with the current international discourse with a view to understanding, as distinct from criticising, the culturally asymmetrical power relations embedded in the international discourse because of the over-representation within it of ideas derived from Western discourses. The difficulty this asymmetry creates is that, whilst international human rights discourse as a mode of social discipline is, and indeed should be, an instance of what Michel Foucault termed 'power/knowledge', it is currently a profoundly biased form of such knowledge that unreasonably narrows the options available to non-Western nations and peoples as they pursue economic and social development.

The second, and more specific, difficulty arises because, in forgetting the Western origins of the discourse, we also forget its imbrication with specific social-structural and institutional forms, and so risk neglecting its dependence on these forms for its enforcement. Thus a tendency has arisen to assume that, once certain rights have been proclaimed, they will be either self-enforcing or automatically enforced by whatever sets of social relations and/or institutions already exist. The difficulty this creates is that we in the West are often very quick to condemn failing states when perhaps we should be criticising ourselves for insisting on development strategies—export-led growth, for example—that undermine established sets of social relations, without either thinking enough about the renewal of existing modes of social defence, or providing for the embedding of the new ones associated with rights discourse. These, then, are the difficulties I will be responding to, although not elaborating on, in the account and discussion of the development of the international human rights regime that follows.

In this chapter, I will deploy Foucault's analytical schema to show how the silence about non-economic social difference and the problem it creates for enforceability, as indexed by the rise of the doctrine of 'justiciability', have been produced within international human rights discourse. The way in which Foucault's schema is used to make sense of the development of human rights discourse, and to diagnose its difficulties both globally and locally, is as follows. First, any specification of a discursive formation is conceived of as a cross-section through the pertinent social conditions at a particular point in time.[1] Secondly, the interactions between the component elements of a discursive formation are understood not so much as a moving equilibrium, but as a shifting agonism whose points of stress and strain as well as modes of suture are determined by its ever-changing rules of formation.

The birth of international human rights discourse

The most obvious point in time at which to cut, so to speak, the first cross-section is 1948, the date of the United Nation's Universal Declaration of Human Rights. The first requirement is to understand why it was that human rights were initially problematised within the institutions of the international system. I know of no braver, more comprehensive (except for the absence of an economic dimension which readers may easily insert for themselves), nor more suitably concise outline of the international and transnational processes involved than that provided by Robertson. I will therefore quote it in full:

> I...propose, in skeletal terms, that the temporal-historical path to the present circumstance of a very high degree of global density and complexity can be delineated as follows:
>
> *Phase I: The Germinal Phase* Lasting in Europe from the early fifteenth until the mid-18th century. Incipient growth of national communities and downplaying of the medieval 'transnational' system. Expanding scope of the Catholic Church. Accentuation of concepts of the individual and of

ideas about humanity. Heliocentric theory of the world and beginning of modern geography; spread of Gregorian calendar.

Phase II: The Incipient Phase Lasting—mainly in Europe—from the mid-18th century until the 1870s. Sharp shift towards the idea of the homogenous, unitary state; crystallization of concepts of formalized international relations, of standardized citizenly individuals and a more concrete conception of humankind. Sharp increases in legal conventions and agencies concerned with international and transnational regulation and communication. International exhibitions. Beginning of problem of 'admission' of non-European societies to 'international society'. Thematization of nationalism-internationalism issue.

Phase III: The Take-off Phase Lasting from the 1870s until the mid-1920s. 'Take-off' here refers to a period during which the increasingly manifest globalizing tendencies of previous periods and places gave way to a single, inexorable form centred upon the four reference points, and thus constraints, of national societies, generic individuals (but with a masculine bias), a single 'international society', and an increasingly singular, but not unified conception of human kind. Early thematization of 'the problem of modernity'. Increasingly global conceptions of the 'correct outline' of an 'acceptable' national society; thematization of ideas concerning national and personal identities; inclusion of a number of non-European societies in 'international society'; international formalization and attempted implementation of ideas about humanity. Globalization of immigration restrictions. Very sharp increase in number and speed of global forms of communication. The first 'international novels'. Rise of ecumenical movement. Development of global competitions—for example the Olympics and Nobel Prizes. Implementation of world time and near global adoption of Gregorian calendar. First World War.

Phase IV: The Struggle-for-Hegemony Phase Lasting from the mid-1920s until the late-1960s. Disputes and wars about the fragile terms of the dominant globalization process established by the end of the take-off period. Establishment of the League of Nations and then the United Nations. Principle of national independence established. Conflicting conceptions of modernity (Allies v the Axis), followed by high point of the Cold War (Conflict within 'the modern project'). Nature of and Prospects for Humanity sharply focused by the Holocaust and use of the atomic bomb. The crystallization of the Third World.

Phase V: The Uncertainty Phase Beginning in the late 1960s and displaying crisis tendencies in the 1990s. Heightening of global consciousness in the late 1960s. Moon landing. Accentuation of 'post-materialist' values. End of the Cold War and manifest rise of the problem of 'rights' and widespread access to nuclear and thermonuclear weaponry. Number of global institutions and movements greatly increases. Sharp acceleration in means of global communication. Societies increasingly face problems of multiculturality and polyethnicity. Conceptions of individuals rendered more complex by gender, sexual, ethnic and racial considerations. Civil

> rights become a global issue. International system more fluid—end of bipolarity. Concern with humankind as a species-community greatly enhanced, particularly via environmental movements. Arising of interest in world civil society and world citizenship, in spite of 'the ethnic revolution'. Consolidation of global media system, including rivalries about such. Islam as a deglobalizing/reglobalizing movement. Earth Summit in Rio de Janeiro (Robertson, 1990, pp 26–27).

Human rights first surfaced as an object of global interest during Robertson's Phase IV. More particularly, after what Francesca Klug (2000, Chapter 4) has described as, for human rights, the 'fallow years' of the inter-war period, it re-surfaced rather tentatively and uncertainly in the course of World War II as part of both the soon to be victorious powers' attempt to alleviate Western guilt concerning the Holocaust, and the planning for a 'People's Peace' (Lauren, 1998, Chapter 6), which had the formation of the United Nations system as its central idea. Accordingly, the critical point one has to understand about the wider global context within which human rights developed is that for most of its existence the discourse has been strongly marked by the subsequent collapse of the victorious alliance, and the emergence of the rivalries, tensions and anxieties that were part of both the Cold War and the decolonisation process (Cassese, 1990; Evans, 1996; Luard, 1982,1989; Sellars, 2002).

The founding text of the UN was its Charter, which, despite the desires of some of its initial signatories, says very little about human rights except that they are important, to be promoted by the UN's Economic and Social Council (ECOSOC), and advanced by international co-operation.[2] In 1946, ECOSOC established a Commission on Human Rights, most of whose members were diplomats who therefore became the premier authorities of delimitation with respect to human rights: it was they who drew up the Universal Declaration. Since the latter document became the definitive grid of specification, and in the light of subsequent tensions over its expansion and the question of whether its component rights are related to one another in any sort of hierarchy, it is important to provide some analysis of its contents. Of the 24 specific human rights listed (Articles 3–26), 18 may be defined as civil and political (see Articles 3–16 and 18–21), six of which concern rights in relation to legal authorities, whilst the remaining six may be defined as economic and social. In other words, this grid took as its object of application capitalist societies wherein private property was sacrosanct (Article 17), the rule of law securely established, the polity liberal-democratic, and there already existed a broad array of social services, voluntary associations, and legal statuses—specifically, social security in all its forms (health, housing, unemployment and old-age insurance, income support, and special protection for mothers and children), education, labour administration, trade unions, and employment contracts.

In line with the way in which human rights became objects of concern, the most important credential for speaking authoritatively about them was identical with the institutional site whence any such speech could emanate, namely representing a 'good' state in the sense of one that possessed the characteristics just listed (cf Marks, 2000, Chapter 2). From the beginning, the UN was divided between 'good' and 'bad' states, in that a small number of states, including the Soviet Union and four of its allies, plus South Africa and Saudi Arabia, had abstained when the Universal Declaration was put to the vote. They did so because they felt that it laid too much stress on the civil and political side. However, reflecting this division and their diplomatic backgrounds, rather than take up any mode of interrogation, the Commission's experts took up a position best summarised as 'see no evil, hear only a little about any evil, and definitely do not speak of any evil'. That is, between 1946 and 1967, and because it claimed to have no such power, the sole body then charged with the task of interrogating states concerning their human rights records refused to investigate any complaints, agreed only to receive very general descriptions of alleged violations for research purposes, and concerned itself with preparing legislation in the form of the later covenants.

Like their specific content, the fact that rights—rather than, say, moral principles—were what the Universal Declaration specified also reflected the social characteristics of the original signatories, although not without tensions. The principal tension was between the proponents of civil and political rights, led by the United States, and those of economic and social principles, led by the Soviet Union, with the Western European and Latin American states in the middle. The result was that the co-existing conceptual and methodological resources upon which the discourse of human rights could draw were divided between those of the law and those of political theory, those of the common and civil law traditions and those of, on the one hand, the great liberal declarations of rights—the Bill of Rights of England's Glorious Revolution, the American Declaration of Independence and Bill of Rights, the French Declaration of the Rights of Man and of the Citizen—and, on the other, the socialist critique of these declarations prefigured and contained in Karl Marx's *On the Jewish Question* and *Critique of the Gotha Programme* respectively. Predictably, given the expertise of the Commission and the impossibility of it doing anything else, the procedure that it initially adopted as its mode of intervention into this new, and from the beginning very complexly structured, field was re-writing. That is, reflecting the divisions between the liberal and the socialist traditions and trying as far as possible to neglect the fact that one of them had the support of some 'bad' states, the Commission spent the eight years from 1946 to 1954 working on what became the two principal Covenants: the International Covenant on Civil and Political Rights (ICCPR) and the International Covenant on Economic, Social and Cultural Rights (ICESCR).

Again reflecting the diversity of the UN's membership, the strategic resources upon which the discourse could draw to define the direction of its development were divided between the same two traditions: a liberal tradition that assumed that citizens were best left to look after themselves, and a socialist one that assumed that they needed or deserved state support. Despite the exclusion of the right to private property from both Covenants, the systematisation or integration of these two thematic authorities was considered to be impossible, so the Commission declared them indivisible and therefore equivalent. However, there was a clear difference between the two strategies as regards their political-economic functionality from the point of view of the majority of 'good' states: the liberal tradition assumed the legitimacy of capitalist economic relations, whilst the socialist tradition was, at the very least, sceptical.

In sum, when one considers this first cross-section through the discursive formation which represented the conditions of possibility of the discourse of human rights at its moment of inception, one can see that it was marked by a significant conceptual division which reflected social-structural differences. However, because of wider asymmetries of wealth, and local ones of voting power, not only were these social-structural differences regarded as non-pertinent, but also the conceptual division took on a moral dimension that significantly reduced the likelihood that the emergent discourse would have any significant economic and social dimension. Nevertheless, the exclusion of private property, the judgmental reticence and drafting activities of the Commission, plus its promulgation of the doctrine of 'indivisibility', meant that the possibility of the discourse gaining such a dimension was not altogether closed-off.

Making human rights enforceable

Because the present argument focuses on the questions of enforcement and enforceability, the most appropriate point in time at which to cut a second cross-section through the discursive formation is 1971, since by that time the UN had become much more interested in such issues. In 1971 the UN was a very different body from what it had been at its inception. In addition to the original 58, the ongoing process of de-colonisation had produced many new members. Moreover, because of the loss of its empire, Britain was no longer the power that it had been, and, because of its unpopular involvement in Vietnam, the United States no longer held the moral high ground, particularly in the eyes of the state-socialist and post-colonial states. Additionally, the economic and political challenges of the 1960s had reinforced the commitment of many Western European states to corporatist social policies that emphasised economic and social entitlements, even as their social-democratic parties retreated from any commitment to socialism as even their ultimate goal. Finally, not only were the former Axis Powers—Japan and West Germany—now members of the UN, but both were clearly on their way to becoming major economic powers. In sum, the Soviet Union and its Eastern European allies, thanks to these developments, their own very erratic reform efforts, and their on/off alliance with China, were no longer either so socially distinctive, so friendless, or so easily anathematised.

As this rather different institutional setting had developed, new authorities of delimitation had gained a greater say and, as a consequence, social, economic and cultural rights secured their place within the grid that specified the nature of human rights as an object of discourse. Thus the two Covenants were not only completed but, in 1966, admittedly after a long delay, submitted for approval by the General Assembly and subsequent ratification by member states. They came into force once the requisite number of ratifications had been obtained, which was in 1976. In Steiner and Alston's (1996, p 126) useful summary, the rights contained within the ICCPR are:

(a) protection of the individual's physical integrity, as in provisions on torture, arbitrary arrest, arbitrary deprivation of life;
(b) procedural fairness when government deprives an individual of liberty, as in provisions on arrest, trial procedure and conditions of imprisonment;
(c) equal protection norms defined in religious, gender and other terms;
(d) freedoms of belief, speech and association, such as provisions on the practice of religion, press freedom, and the right to hold assembly and form associations; and
(e) the right to political participation.

Likewise, the central provisions of the ICESCR may be briefly summarised as:

(a) the right of self-determination;
(b) the rights to work, just and favourable conditions at work, and the right to form and join trade unions;
(c) the rights to social security, family and mother/child support, and protection in childhood;
(d) the rights to an adequate standard of living, physical and mental health, and education;
(e) the rights to cultural participation, knowledge and copyright;
(f) equal protection norms defined in religious, gender, racial, and other terms.

Moreover, the credentials for speaking authoritatively about them became more inclusive as the definition of a 'good' state was simultaneously broadened. Thus the notion of the 'indivisibility' of the two sets of rights gained more substance not only because their more detailed specification made it easier to see that they at least overlapped, but also because a practical, rather than principled, rationale was agreed for their continuing separation, namely the distinction between 'justiciable' civil and political rights and 'programmatic' economic and social rights. This practical, Isaiah Berlin-inspired rationale was provided in the official annotations to the draft texts of the two covenants:

> Those in favour of drafting two separate covenants argued that *civil and political rights were enforceable, or justiciable, or of an 'absolute' character, while economic, social and cultural rights were not or might not be; that the former were immediately applicable, while the latter were to be progressively implemented;* and that, generally speaking, the former were rights of the individual 'against' the state...while the latter were rights which the state would have to take positive action to promote... The question of drafting one or two covenants was intimately related to the question of implementation... Since the rights could be divided into two broad categories,

> which should be subject to different procedures of implementation, it would be both logical and convenient to formulate two separate covenants (quoted in Steiner and Alston, 1996, p 261, emphasis added).

This move in the direction of consensus was accompanied by a similarly explainable move in the direction of more active modes of interrogation of the membership's behaviour as regards the human rights of their citizens—the UN now listened far more attentively, and it began to question and look. This process had begun in 1959, when ECOSOC (Resolution 28) repeated its invitation to the citizens of member states to communicate any complaints to the Secretary General. In 1967, ECOSOC (Resolution 1235) had sanctioned a decision by the Human Rights Commission to engage in an annual public debate on any gross violations known to it and also, if necessary, to engage in thorough studies of such violations with a view to making recommendations both to the state concerned and, again if necessary, to one or other of the UN organs for further action.

Three years later, in 1970, ECOSOC (Resolution 1503) had further authorised its Sub-Commission on the Prevention of Discrimination and Protection of Minorities to consider complaints concerning gross violations and any governmental responses already received under conditions of confidentiality, and with a view to ascertaining whether or not they indeed revealed 'a consistent pattern of gross and reliably attested violations of human rights...within [its] terms of reference' (quoted in Steiner and Alston, 1996, p 376). In cases where the Sub-Commission feels there is cause for concern, it is empowered to refer them to the Commission on Human Rights for detailed study with a view to the Commission making recommendations to other UN organs, again under conditions of confidentiality, unless it decides to transfer the issue to the public 1235 procedure.

Finally, a state's ratification of either or both of the general covenants means that, according to international law, and as signatories of treaties rather than simply the supporters of a declaration (even though support for the Universal Declaration on Human Rights is required as a condition of membership), they incur binding legal obligations in respect of the content of the covenants. The first of these obligations is the quinquennial filing of reports on implementation with the Human Rights Committee created by the ICCPR—a committee whose members were initially and remain largely lawyers, and the far more tardily formed Committee on Economic, Social and Cultural Rights. These reports are then considered by the relevant committee, which returns them with its own comments, criticisms and requests for further information, or supplementary reports, in the hope of stimulating improved performance. Signatories to the First Optional Protocol to the ICCPR, which allows their citizens to make direct complaints to the Committee, also incur the obligation to at least receive the Committee's 'Views' of the complaint. All of these requirements and procedures also apply to signatories to the Convention on the Elimination of Racial Discrimination (CERD), which was approved by the General Assembly in 1965 and came into force in 1969.

Concerning the conceptual dimension of the discursive formation around 1971, here too things were rather different as compared to around 1946, and the partial equalisation of the balance of power between the proponents of the civil/political and the social/economic approaches played an important part. But also important was the role of legal discourse in reducing the conceptual antagonism between these approaches. As well as the legal expertise located in the Human Rights Committee, legal concepts and ways of thinking gradually displaced political ones in the UN's handling of human rights issues (Rancharan, 1997). This is particularly clear in the way that the Committee made, and was allowed to make, international law through its General Comments, which address not simply procedural issues associated with the improvement of the quality of the reports they receive, but also bear on issues of interpretation with respect to the meanings of articles and the criteria for proper implementation. Also, the investigations and reports or 'Views' under Resolutions 1235 and 1503, as well as the responses to individual complaints allowed by the First Optional Protocol, took on an increasingly judicial cast. The net result was that much of the activity undertaken during the 1970s may be summarised as the transcribing of politically inspired texts into legal language. Thus, and at least in relation to the ICCPR and the ICESCR, legal modes of reasoning and principles became the chief strategic resource defining the future direction of the human rights project. As a result, not only were Liberalism and Socialism displaced as such resources, but also the issues of their respective relationships to human rights were shelved. This, like the earlier exclusion of the right to private property from the ICCPR and the ICESCR, latterly proved to be politically functional as the détente between the super-powers developed.

In sum, when one considers this second cross-section, one can see that the conceptual division that was such a marked feature of the first one had been transmuted into a legally expressed set of differences of purpose and modes of implementation. In this way, then, the initial reticence of the Commission paid off in terms of allowing a consensus to emerge and active enforcement to begin. However, this also meant that the social-structural differences implicit in divergent political ideologies tended to disappear from human rights discourse as in any way pertinent to the issue of enforcement. Moreover, the fact that they disappeared in a largely capitalist world, whether measured numerically or in terms of the distribution of economic resources, and that the medium through which they disappeared was that of liberal Western law, meant that economic and social rights were about to encounter a new challenge to their status within the pantheon of rights. This challenge is summarised by the term 'justiciability': the requirement that for a right to be properly so called, judicial remedies must be available where violations occur. The nature of this challenge, and as it happens, a neat exemplification of how this discussion remains bedevilled by a confusion of economic rights in particular with rights to substantial material benefits, is very clearly indicated in the following quotation from a globally influential source:

> Describing paid holidays as a basic human right (as the Universal Declaration does in Article 24) just seems wrong headed... Claims for economic goods are not

> justiciable. A court of law, even in a poor country, can determine when civil and political rights are being violated by the government, but it cannot, by a mere legal judgement, summon the resources to meet social and economic goals (*The Economist*, 5 December 1998, p 9; see also, more surprisingly, O'Neill, 2002, p 28).

The juridification of human rights discourse

Once again reflecting the present argument's focus on questions of enforcement and enforceability, 1990 would seem the most appropriate point at which to cut the third and final cross-section through the discursive formation, since by then the present array of institutions and processes was in place. However, the human rights project was also by this time in a state of some crisis. The weakening and eventual collapse of the Soviet Union had allowed tensions that had been suppressed by the realpolitik of the Cold War to come to the surface in the form of a strong reassertion by some states of the pertinence of, and the challenges posed by, social-structural differences. The source of this crisis was the tension created by the simultaneous occurrence of three developments that affected the play of forces within the institutional site represented by the UN system: the increased influence of largely Western-based Non-Governmental Organisations (NGOs, and International Non-Governmental Organisations (INGOs) committed to enlarging and deepening the ambit of human rights discourse; the rise of neo-liberalism in the United States and Britain in particular; and the increased cultural assertiveness of many Asian states as some insisted on their Islamic culture, others drew confidence from their economic achievements, and China became more engaged in global and UN politics (Bauer and Bell, 1999; Davis, 1995; Langlois, 2001; Tang, 1995; Woodiwiss, 1998).

The NGOs and INGOs were successful in that the 1979 Convention on the Elimination of all Forms of Discrimination against Women (CEDAW) became effective in 1981, the 1984 Convention against Torture (CAT) in 1985, and the 1989 Convention on the Rights of the Child (CRC) in 1990. However, the effect of these conventions was somewhat reduced by the simultaneous development of resistances on two fronts. The first was represented by some Western nations rejecting any pressure on them to enhance economic and social rights: not only did the Reagan and Bush Administrations continue to refuse to contemplate the ratification of the ICESCR, but they also suspended the ratification process of the ICCPR that the Carter Administration had initiated. The second was that represented by some Asian states' equally strong rejection of any insistence on the enhancement of civil and political rights. In the first case, resistance was justified by the economic success of an unshackled capitalism and the political victory of liberal democracy over socialism. In the second, most powerfully expressed in the 1993 Bangkok Government Declaration which preceded the UN's Second World Conference on Human Rights held later the same year in Vienna, untrammelled liberal democracy was seen as an obstacle to the achievement of the same economic success and therefore to the advancement of economic and social rights, whilst certain aspects of the project to enhance women's rights in particular were regarded as culturally imperialistic. In sum, the geopolitics of the 1980s produced two new claimants to positions amongst the authorities of delimitation—the NGO movement and certain Asian governments, but without any accompanying challenges to either the basic grid of specification concerning the object of human rights discourse or the conceptual or strategic resources of human rights work at the UN level.

In terms of the pertinent 'enunciative modalities', the credentials and institutional locations required for authoritative speech had become more inclusive as the wider but predominantly Western legal and NGO communities were recognised. However, those of the 'Asian values' constituency were refused. In the words of the implicitly dismissive Vienna Declaration of 1993:

> ...All human rights are universal, indivisible and independent and interrelated ...While the significance of national and regional particularities and various historical, cultural and religious backgrounds must be borne in mind, it is the duty of States, regardless of their political, economic and cultural systems, to promote and protect all human rights and fundamental freedoms (quoted in Steiner and Alston, 1996, p 235).

In the meantime, the interrogation of the human rights records of the signatories to the growing number of covenants—signatories which still did not include the United States and China—had become even more detailed and insistent, consequent not only on the steadily improving administrative and legal rigour of the procedures involved, but also on the increased access granted to NGOs—by 1994, 900 NGOs had official consultative status with the UN, whilst 1,500 were represented at the Vienna Conference. Thus not only did the Committees set up under the various conventions become more demanding and critical with respect to the content of the reports that had to be filed with them, but the number of complaints they received grew exponentially—'until the mid-1980s the UN received, on average, 25,000 complaints per year. Recently this number has ballooned to around 300,000, but many of these complaints are identical as a result of letter-writing campaigns by groups with a large and active membership' (Steiner and Alston, 1996, p 380). Moreover, not only was the appointment of rapporteurs empowered to make site visits added to the range of methods of fact-finding available to the committees, but also 'thematic mechanisms' were instituted by the Commission, which provide for the continuing monitoring of areas of concern by either working groups or special rapporteurs. In 1995, 13 such mechanisms were in operation. They were concerned with: disappearances, arbitrary detention, extra-judicial executions, freedom of expression, racial discrimination, torture, religious intolerance, use of mercenaries, commercial sexual abuse of children, internally displaced persons, judicial independence, violence against women, and the effects of toxic and dangerous products on human rights.

With respect to the conceptual dimension of the discursive formation circa 1990, and although political concepts, such as those associated with feminism, informed some of the campaigns for the new covenants, legal discourse became ever more entrenched as the source of concepts to think through difficulties as well as to more generally 'handle' human rights issues. Furthermore, the various committees became ever more confidently judicial in their reasoning and the tone of their comments and Views' (McGoldrick, 1991). Thus even the once formidable barrier to the jurisdiction of the UN's human rights institutions represented by national sovereignty was overcome, legally at least, as Louis Sohn (1994) and Steiner and Alston (1996, pp 369–72) have shown in their accounts of the UN's relations with the previous regimes in South Africa and Poland respectively (see also Mills, 1998). This development was buttressed by the emergence of regional human rights jurisdictions in the forms of the European Court of Human Rights, the African Commission on Human and Peoples' Rights, and the Inter-American Court for Human Rights. Less positively, it is also illustrated by the rather imperious way in which the doctrine of indivisibility was used to dismiss the 'Asian values' argument in the extract from the Vienna Declaration quoted above. Thus legal and political discourses now co-exist under the terms established by the hegemony of the legal discourse, with the result that even the proponents of politically inspired arguments can only hope to make a difference if they use legal terms or, minimally, do not challenge legal norms or procedures—legal reasoning, then, is now virtually the only possible way of working within the conceptual field of human rights.

In these ways, then, legal reason became firmly established as not simply the principal conceptual resource, but the principal strategic resource too. Thus it today defines the future of human rights not just as regards the development of the extant covenants and conventions, but also as regards any possible new treaties, in that unfortunately all now have to pass the current exclusionary variant of the 'justiciability' test. The functionality of all this for the geopolitical position of the United States was graphically borne out by the role of human rights discourse, in the form of the 1975 Helsinki Accords, during the latter days of the Soviet Empire:

> Whatever contribution the process ultimately made to the demise of Communism, it clearly played an important role, especially in the second half of the 1980s and the early 1990s, in legitimating human rights discourse within Eastern Europe, providing a focus for non-governmental activities at both the domestic and international levels...(Steiner and Alston, 1996, p 578).

As will be explained in the concluding chapter, the opening of the 21st century has, rather surprisingly, seen the functionality of legal reason for its global position carelessly undermined by the United States as it has prosecuted its War on Terrorism.

Conclusion

Putting to one side what we must hope is the American government's temporary desertion of the human rights cause, all this is as it should be, except, as I will argue below, that justiciability should also be a requirement with respect to rights under the ICESCR rather than its presumed impossibility being a mode of diminishing them. For all its faults and limitations, the law and its enforcing institutions are undoubtedly the best means humanity has yet developed for endeavouring to ensure that people are non-violently protected from state, and indeed mutual, oppression when this is necessary. Moreover, now that at last the United States has ratified at least the ICCPR and China has signed the ICESCR and promised to sign the ICCPR, the human rights regime has a truly global reach. However, at least one major problem remains to be properly addressed in the area of enforcement, and that is the broader and sociological question of the fit between human rights law and the particularities of global social relations. This arises because the legal discourse of human rights still takes as its object of application at the national level the same kind of social structure that it did in the 1940s; namely capitalist societies where individualism is a significant component of the value system, the rule of law is securely established, the polity is liberal-democratic and there exists a broad array of social services, voluntary associations, and widely recognised legal statuses. Indeed, the taken-for-granted character of this specification of the national object of application has been still further enhanced by developments both within the discourse of human rights and amongst its conditions of existence. The principal instance of the first is the well-established view that not only economic and social rights, but also some civil and political ones too, notably those pertaining to access to the legal system, are programmatic rather than absolute or 'justiciable' in character; that is, the obligations that states parties incur with respect to economic and social rights are more to make progress in achieving certain goals of a largely institutional character than to provide for enforcement. The pertinent development with respect to conditions of existence was, of course, the demise of socialism in Russia and Eastern Europe.

There is an irony inherent in the distinction between justiciable civil/ political and programmatic economic/social rights. And it is that, although it was intended to help those in need, it in fact discriminates against them. Thus it was introduced, in what one must assume was good faith, so as not to impose too great an economic burden on developing societies, and because economic and social rights are for some reason thought to be more expensive to implement than civil and political ones—the latter merely require imposing buildings, well-found offices and princely salaries for politicians and legal personnel for their implementation. Such reasoning is, however, profoundly mistaken since, and as Marshall (1994) made clear so long ago and indeed the Economic, Social and Cultural Rights Committee has more recently attested in one of its 'general comments' (Alston, 1992, p 495), the discourse of what Marshall termed 'social citizenship rights' is concerned with procedurally establishing equality of status with regard to certain minimum material conditions, rather than the equalisation of material conditions that many of the proponents of the narrow reading of justiciability seem to fear. Moreover, the ICESCR (Article 2) only requires states parties to deploy 'the *maximum available* resources' (emphasis added). Thus to say that even such minimal and cheaply deliverable (Sen, 1999b) entitlements as many labour rights and a right to 'adequate housing', for example, are not justiciable cannot mean that they could not in principle be pursued through the courts, since all such a possibility would require would be appropriately drafted legislation, for which many models exist in the statute books and administrative regulations of the more developed societies. Rather, what it does mean is that there is no UN requirement for the existence of such legislation. One result is that any response to need is therefore left to the discretion of governments and their calculations of political advantage without any danger that a court might make an order that, for example, ultimately required them to forego some of their expensive, state-provided cars in favour of sheets of corrugated-iron roofing to be distributed amongst those in need. Another result is that, since Article 1 of the ICESCR defines resources to include those made available 'through international assistance and co-operation, especially economic and technical', there is also no possibility that the richer countries could be held to account with respect to the level of assistance they provide.

Thus the West's insistence on justiciability as a necessary quality of 'real rights' should also be understood in the context of its strenuous resistance to such globally redistributive rights as those to development and freedom of information. Tragically, the distinction therefore catches many millions of people in the less developed countries in a vicious double bind. This double bind arises for the following reasons. First, because of the artificial narrowing of what is considered to be justiciable, many are currently deprived of legal remedies with respect to violations of certain civil and political as well as economic, social and cultural rights (Genugten and Perez-Bustillo, 2001). Secondly, the coverage of human rights discourse is now so broad, and its requirements so institutionally specific, in many ways rightly so, and, less justifiably, Western-inspired, that it reaches deep into the inner recesses of social structures, where the social routines pertaining to human rights are not simply interconnected with many others, but depend upon them for their functioning. Thus, because of the discourse's implicit evolutionism, the only way in which, to use Jeffrey Harrod's (1987) term, the 'unprotected' will gain full access to their rights is when the societies in which they live reach Western levels of development. However, it cannot be assumed, as the concept of programmatic rights implicitly suggests, that in time, and as they develop, all of them will or should converge on the kind of 'modern' society that the specification of the object of application instances, namely a prosperous, market-driven economy, a liberal polity, and an individualistic value system (Woodiwiss, 2001a, Chapter 4). This is for two main reasons: (1) the operation of the global economic system is as likely to prevent development in some societies as it is to encourage it; (2) the environing social and economic routines are often culturally specific, very different from those associated with the supposed 'modern' archetype (see below, Chapter 4), and presumably protected by both the right to self-determination as developed in the UN's 1970 Declaration on Friendly Relations and, by implication at least, the much more recent acknowledgment of indigenous rights.

In sum, the double bind that many people in less developed societies find themselves in, thanks to the narrow construction of justiciability, is as follows: first, they are currently denied rights that according to international law are theirs, and which, as I will show in Chapter 4, are far more readily socially embeddable than certain civil rights; secondly, they will only be able to enjoy them in the future if they sacrifice much that they value in their cultures and the quality of their social relations. However, if they make such sacrifices it may well be that their lives will become less secure thanks to the breaking of many of the social ties upon which, for all their imperfections, they currently depend to protect themselves from the arbitrariness of the powerful and the vagaries of fate (on the general point, see Zhang Yimou's film *Qui Ju* and Taylor, 1999; also, for a discussion of some attempts to re-invent 'traditional' protections under such headings as 'restorative justice', see Broadhurst, 1999). Moreover, what has made them even more vulnerable is the fact that the version of democracy—'low intensity democracy'—currently sanctioned by international human rights law is very narrowly procedural (Marks, 2000, Chapters 2 and 3), resting as it does on a 'new global constitutionalism' (Schneiderman, 2000) developed in the sphere of international private law. This 'constitutionalism' has filled the gap created by the UN Covenants' silence concerning private property by privileging property rights over all others, and therefore means that the world's poorest citizens have little hope of future economic and social support.

How, then, might the victims of this double bind be released? Two steps seem to be essential. The first is to establish the justiciability of economic and social rights and facilitate their enforcement by extending the procedures for intervention in human rights discourse to allow the pertinent UN institutions to engage in a limited process of sociologically informed conceptual translation between the two sets of rights. The second is to challenge, through support for the addition of a 'social clause' to the protocols of the World Trade Organization, the common view that economic and social rights are not justiciable at the international level, since it is this view that allows the decision as to their justiciability to be left to the discretion of governments. My suggestion, then, is that in these ways, amongst many others no doubt, international human rights discourse might yet be made to be more truly multilingual and so overcome its constructed silence with respect to social difference, and so move closer to becoming an achieved instance of cosmopolis.

Notes

1 This said, no such cross-section can be clean-cut, so to speak. This is because some of the elements of a discursive formation consist of diachronic or change-making processes that have their effects over a number of years. I have dealt with this problem by discussing such processes in relation to what appeared to me to be the most appropriate point in time, whether their principal effects precede or succeed it.

2 My aim in this chapter is to make a series of analytical points. Thus I make no claims to empirical novelty. Indeed, virtually all of the factual material has been very parsimoniously derived from a small number of texts, namely the histories by Cassese (1990), Evans (1996), Lauren (1998), Luard (1982; 1989), Morsink (1999), Sellars (2002), Tolley (1987), and Vincent (1986), the comprehensive volume of texts and materials by Steiner and Alston (1996), and texts on enforcement by Alston (1992), Alston and Crawford (2000), and Flood (1998). Readers desiring further information, discussion and suggestions for further reading concerning many of the points or arguments made in this chapter, or indeed the many that have been neglected, should easily be able to find what they are looking for by consulting these excellent resources.

Chapter 3
The plural forms of labour rights and the possibility of translation

The purpose of this and the following chapter is to demonstrate the possibility and, indeed, the necessity of socio-legal translation as a new mode of working within the international human rights regime. This argument will be made by analysing the development of labour rights in a wide variety of different societies.[1] The argument is divided into two parts. The first part, set out in the present chapter, seeks to establish the possibility of the translation enterprise by showing that, outside the United States, there are many labour rights regimes in the West that do not privilege the civil and political right of freedom of association, but have been constituted instead by the translation of, to use Hohfeld's vocabulary, the liberties' entailed by an untrammeled right to freedom of association into various 'claims' and 'powers' in the form of economic and social rights. Not only have such translations proved acceptable, and therefore been democratically approved in a wide variety of societies, but they may also be seen to have been more effective at protecting labour in particular social contexts than might have been the case had the translations not taken place. The second part of the argument, set out in the following chapter, begins by presenting an ideal type of what an effective human rights regime would look like in a familialist society, outlines the development of labour rights regimes in a number of broadly familialist societies, and specifies the strategic options that are opened for the embedding and enforcing of human rights in Asia and the South more generally, once the idea of the non-justiciable nature of economic and social rights has been laid to rest.

Liberal democracy, socialism and labour rights

Perhaps the best-known attempt to give a narrative form to, or periodise, the development of labour rights and their relationship to the wider society is that produced by Franz Neumann in the 1920s, and introduced to an English-speaking audience by Otto Kahn-Freund in the 1940s. According to Kahn-Freund (1944; see also Jacobs, 1986), labour law systems typically pass through three phases—repression, toleration and recognition—reflecting the developing but never complete equalisation of class balances.[2] As all who have used this periodisation have pointed out, if applied too mechanically, it is an excessively optimistic, Anglo-centric and evolutionistic schematisation. Nevertheless, when separated from these evolutionistic connotations, the schematisation provides a defensible and useful vocabulary for talking comparatively about different phases in the development of labour law systems.

What I therefore intend to do here are two things. First, I will show how my Hohfeldian conception of rights enables one to at least map, and so render more intelligible, the character of some aspects of the complex social wholes of which labour rights are always parts, as well as of the nature of the differing rhythms, orderings (including reversals), and class-structural significances of the histories which I will summarise. As explained above (p 15), for Hohfeld, rights comprise a set of four distinguishable and partially mutually substitutable clusters of liberties and/or entitlements that may be used to qualify class relations within the employment sphere: 'liberties' to perform certain actions; 'claims' or expectations vis à vis specified others; 'powers' that allow legal subjects to assume certain specified roles and change certain social relations; and 'immunities' against prosecution and/or civil suit in the pursuit of ends that would otherwise be regarded as illegal. Secondly, I will specify what I consider to be the significance of this account for labour law reform today, particularly with respect to what it implies with respect to the strategies that might be pursued in order to redress imbalances in employment relations not only in the 'South', but also and *therefore* in the North, too.

In order to reduce repetition, as well as to provide at least a tacit acknowledgment of certain critical differences with respect to levels of development, social structures and transnational conditions of existence, I will divide my highly schematic discussion of the histories with which I am concerned into three groups: first, the early industrialisers (Britain, the United States and France); second, the earliest wave of 'late' industrialisers (Sweden, Canada, Australia and Japan); and third, the post-1945 industrialisers (Argentina, Brazil, Taiwan, Hong Kong and Singapore).[3] The first two groups minus Japan will be discussed in this chapter, whilst Japan, for reasons to be explained below, and the third group will be discussed in the following chapter.

Early industrialisers

The first laws specifically applied to capitalist wage labour in Britain and its former colony, the United States, were the British Combination Acts of 1799 and 1800. Yet, far from altering the class balances to labour's advantage, these Acts merely generalised some earlier, more narrowly targeted punitive statutes, despite the establishment of a compulsory arbitration procedure (labour had no say in the choice of arbitrators). Thus they had as their desired effect the prevention of combinations of labourers from organising and acting to enhance their positions with respect to, in Jones' terminology (see note 1 above, p 20), possession and control, and therefore undermining the prerogatives of title with respect to the disposition of any surplus arising from production. The partial repeal of the original Combination Acts—in the form of the 1825 Combination Act in Britain and an 1842 decision by Massachusetts Justice Lemuel Shaw (*Commonwealth v Hunt*, 4 Metc 3) in the United States—meant that what unions there were, far fewer in both countries in the second quarter of the 19th century than in the first, no longer committed a criminal offence by their simple existence. However, not only did the increased tempo of industrialisation and recurrent recessions make it difficult for unions to survive, but they also found that their freedom to bargain over wages and conditions made little difference to their possessory or control positions. This was because they lacked any legal means of exerting pressure on employers, since picketing and striking, for example, were most often found by judges to instance the 'Violence', 'threats', 'molestation', 'intimidation', or 'obstruction' still forbidden by the 1825 Act and the Massachusetts decision. Moreover, when unions did begin to reappear in the 1850s in Britain, individual strikers knew that they could easily be prosecuted for breach of contract. Interestingly, this was not quite the case when unions reappeared in the 1870s in the United States, where a rather different, newer and more obviously ideological fault—which I have termed 'breach of freedom of contract'—had first to be invented (Woodiwiss, 1990b, pp 42ff and 89ff). Contra Karen Orren (1991), who sees the possibility of such a breach as a feudal survival, this seems to have been necessary because of the more expansive meaning given to contractual freedom during the first three quarters of the 19th century in the much less feudal society of the United States. However, even the brief juridical hiatus in the interim before this regressive development was produced provided only short-lived and cold relative comfort to American trade unionists. This was because their British counterparts were by then enjoying the new freedoms granted by the Trade Union Act (1871) and the Conspiracy and Protection of Property Act (1875), whilst American trade unionists were about to become the victims of 'government by injunction'.

The British Acts of 1871 and 1875 for the first time gave unions some financial security, positively sanctioned their non-violent resort to strikes and picketing, and therefore allowed them certain 'liberties' to contest capital's possessory and control positions. Thus British labour law entered the phase that Kahn-Freund termed 'toleration', in that labour was allowed to seek whatever alterations to the balances between itself and capital that its industrial muscle allowed. In the event, such alterations were minimal because of a whole host of wider social-structural conditions that prevented labour from taking immediate advantage of its 'liberties'. What is more, the 'liberties' themselves soon lost much of their allure, since under certain far from rare conditions their exercise could result in the bankrupting of a union. This was because of the judicial development of civil liability in tort with respect to trade disputes, as a result of which unions could be sued for damages by companies that suffered as a result of their actions.

However, by the time of the House of Lords' *Taff Vale* judgment of 1901, which confirmed the legality of such suits, the wider social-structural conditions had changed still more—but this time to labour's advantage. Unions had spread beyond their traditional constituency of skilled workers to organise many of the unskilled as well as the new category of the semi-skilled. But, perhaps most importantly, labour had become a political force that warranted respect. Hence the passage of the 1906 Trade Disputes Act, which initiated the phase of recognition not by the grant of any more explicitly or rigorously defined 'liberties', but rather by the grant of 'immunities' with respect to what would otherwise be regarded as actionable wrongs. Up to the present, the alterations to local workplace balances between labour and capital produced by the resulting system of 'collective laissez-faire' have varied according to the scope subsequently allowed to the 'immunities'. These variations have occurred according to a rhythm determined by labour's variable access to political power. They have also been accompanied by a similarly determined ebb and flow of statutory claim rights inscribed within individual employment contracts, imposing various obligations on employers, government social policies, and grants of participative 'powers' to set wage levels and/or otherwise determine employment conditions in national tripartite bodies. The latter, like the economically determined alterations, were largely restricted to possessory relations, but did sometimes relate to title-related issues when questions of taxation, nationalisation and privatisation were involved. The net effect, however, has been the gradual translation of the freedoms allowed by the original 'immunities' into entitlements in the form of 'claims' and, less often, 'powers' vis à vis employers and the state.

By contrast, very little in the way of such translation has occurred in the United States, for reasons that will now be explained. Picking up the story in the late 19th century, American labour law slipped back from a phase that has been characterised as one of 'reluctant tolerance' (Lieberman, 1950) to one of repression, thanks to the rise of the labour injunction as an anti-strike weapon in the last quarter of the 19th century. Although this device was made possible by very similar juridical developments to those which made a trade dispute a possible occasion of civil injury in Britain, it was more directly repressive in that disobeying such an injunction carried the threat of imprisonment for contempt of court; also an injunction could be invoked during or even before a dispute took place rather than afterwards, as in the case of the British tort action. Thus, whenever it was invoked, it instantly negated all 'liberties', since as a judicial order to 'cease and desist' it had its effect at the level of control relations. This negation had particularly inequitable consequences because the constitutional backing that the American courts gave to their own law-making had also permitted the striking down of previous legislative efforts to inscribe any possessory 'claims' in contracts of employment. Moreover, wider social-structural differences characteristic of the United States as distinct from Britain—a narrowly based labour movement, an ethnically and racially divided labour force, and a minimal labour presence in politics—not only contributed to judicial supremacy, but explain why this assault on labour's 'liberties' and denial of any 'claim rights' did not initiate the successful counter movement that it did in Britain.

In the absence of any such response in the United States, labour was left to make what use it could of its fragile remaining 'liberties', which was not much. However, in contrast to Britain, these 'liberties' were eventually explicitly defined in law thanks to the passage of the Wagner Act in 1935—but not in response to any demand from labour. Rather, they were a grudgingly accepted gift from a politically needy but neither socialist nor even labourist Democratic Party. Unsurprisingly, the courts rapidly restricted the ambit of the 'liberties'—notably that to collective bargaining—that the Wagner Act had granted to the sphere of possessory relations. A rapidly produced doctrine of 'the managerial prerogative' meant that most control issues were non-negotiable, whilst labour's lack of political clout meant that few 'claims' against either employers or the state were statutorily inscribed within employment contracts. In addition, labour's non-socialist character meant that it sought few if any participative 'powers' to change employment conditions, whilst title has seldom been a public issue even under the heading of taxation, since there was no demand for the state to distribute any more than a minimum of social benefits. All the same, title has over the last two decades proved to be a 'local' issue in an increasing and now significant number of companies, as they have sought either increased capitalisation or escape from bankruptcy during recessions through the establishment of Employee Share Ownership Plans (ESOPS).

However, the legal enforceability of collective contracts, the fact that they include as bargained 'claims' on the company many of the items that are statutorily defined 'claims' on the state in Britain, as well as no-strike and arbitration clauses, mean that the conditions under which even possessory 'liberties' can be asserted through industrial action of any kind have become very limited—too much is at risk. Startlingly, as Katherine Stone (1999) has made clear, the take-up of union-negotiated 'claims' on companies—in relation to unfair dismissal, for example—now excludes their recipients from access to the currently increasing quantum of statutorily established possessory 'claims' on the state. The latter are therefore not an automatically inscribed set of minima in all employment contracts, to be improved upon through collective negotiation, as is the case in Western Europe. They instead function as an incentive to de-unionisation and therefore to sacrificing any remaining collectively exercisable 'liberties' to challenge even capital's possessory power.

Turning to France, one encounters a history where the central state plays a far more important role in societal governance than in either the United States or Britain. As a consequence, the critical dimension of employment relations is its political or control dimension, and therefore the critical modality of legal regulation is that of 'powers'—or what the French call 'police'—rather than 'liberties' or 'immunities', either in themselves or as the source of 'claims' in individual or collective contracts. What is significant in the present context is not so much that, as it happens, this has been to the benefit of labour, but that morphologically the history of labour law in France is more or less the mirror image of that of the United States. One sign, and indeed a great facilitator, of the greater role of the state in France is the codified and rational nature of the legal system. This, however, does not mean that a phase of toleration or, indeed, ambiguity is absent from the history of French collective labour law any more than it is absent from the history of French industrial relations. Rather, the willingness and, indeed, inability or unwillingness of the state to exercise its power has meant that the history of French labour law is a history of ambivalence.

Thus, although the period 1791 to 1864 may be clearly defined as one of repression, this does not mean that freedom of contract was sacrosanct. It is true that, as Bernard Edelman (1979) has made particularly clear, private property is the core assumption of the Civil Code and, as Norbert Olszak (1999) has explained, this meant that for a long time there was no way in which collective action could be recognised as legal. This said, from the beginning, the state allowed the possibility that, if it so wished, it could continue to exercise its power to inscribe certain 'claims' in some individual contracts of employment where safety or some national interest might be at stake. The state was also willing to delegate some of its powers to 'boards of masters and men' in order to regulate wages, which it did with widely varying degrees of success. However, the state was not entirely free to decide on either the disposition or range of its powers. And, even after the commencement of the recognition phase in 1884, the courts refused to accept that terms agreed in the course of collective bargaining automatically applied to the individual contracts of those covered by the negotiations.

Because of labour's political weight—as in Britain and in contrast to the United States, and in the absence of a solution via the judiciary—a legislative solution to the problem of the automatic extension of collective bargaining, and therefore to that of how 'liberties' were to be translated into 'claims, was provided by laws passed in 1906, 1919 and 1920 which, in the end, extended any benefits won in national negotiations to the entire labour force of the enterprises concerned. In strong contrast to what was happening in Britain and the United States, as a result of the Matignon Accords negotiated under the Popular Front Government in 1936, the scope of negotiations and their applicability were both hugely extended so that they became sectorally and/or geographically binding. However, in 1938 the state reasserted its interest in the outcomes of such otherwise private negotiations in a way that paved the way for the establishment of the Vichy government's despotic form of corporatism.

In 1950, the pre-Vichy 1936 system was restored, and in 1971 it was given more robust foundation by the declaration that collective labour rights were at base individual rights. The latter change gave a new emphasis to local bargaining, as the regional and sectoral institutions created by the delegation of state power have apparently atrophied or become moribund. In sum, looking backwards from the present, the French trajectory may be seen formally as the reverse of that in the US: that is, it has been a movement from a system based on public 'powers' to one based on private 'liberties'. But it would be misleading to see the substantive effect as a convergence between the French and United States systems. The state-inscribed 'claims' in French employment contracts and on the state remain far, far more extensive and significant than in the United States. And not the least of the reasons for this is that political or control relations continue to have far greater salience for employment relations in France than in the United States, despite all the neo-liberal-inspired efforts to privatise not just nationalised industries, but economic life as a whole—the Jospin government's introduction of a 35 hour week during the 1990s was a particularly dramatic illustration of this difference.

Late industrialisers

There has even been talk of privatisation in the country where the translation of 'liberties' into economic and social 'claims' has been taken furthest—namely Sweden. Thus far, however, there is little sign of a significant re-structuring of Swedish labour law. The history of this labour law, if not the wider history of Swedish industrial relations, does not fit the Neumann/Kahn-Freund model as it does not include clear periods of either repression or toleration, since trade unions only appeared after the promulgation of the 1866 Constitution which contained a general right to freedom of association. Thus Swedish unions were at no time regarded as either intrinsically criminal or, as in France, a legal impossibility, even though incitement to strike was an offence in Sweden. However, despite its absolutist past, its monarchical form and its codified legal system, the Swedish state was at first very reticent about both the exercise and the delegation of its power. Thus, prior to the 1930s, the state acted neither to legalise nor prohibit the industrial actions that can make freedom of association into a potent industrial weapon. Nor, indeed, did it pass much legislation to protect vulnerable workers. Consequently, like Britain and the United States but unlike France, employment relations revolved around the possessory dimension and, legally, labour's 'liberties' were pitted against those of capital.

Even when the state did intervene in a significant way following the December Compromise of 1906 between the unions and the employers association, it did so in the same reticent manner—that is, by passing the Mediation Act in which the state offered, but did not require the acceptance of, its good offices to aid the conflicting parties in coming to an agreement. Similarly, when the Arbitration Act was passed in 1920, it too provided for a voluntary process. State compulsion entered Swedish industrial relations only in 1928, when a conservative government removed contract disputes from the private to the juridical domain through the Collective Contracts Act and the Labour Court Act. In 1932, the Social Democrats began their four uninterrupted decades in power, but not only did they refuse to repeal these two Acts, they also passed the Collective Bargaining Act in 1936, which required new unions to register with the Social Welfare Board if they were to be granted negotiating rights. The *quid pro quo* for the unions' acceptance of the diminution of their 'liberties' represented by the juridification of most aspects of industrial relations was twofold. First, they were translated into a 43 comprehensive social welfare programme, and secondly, in 1938, they were translated into the procedures specified in the core text defining the Swedish industrial relations system—the Basic Agreement. The net result was, and remains, a system of labour law still focused on possessory relations wherein the state uses its power to inscribe certain minimal 'claims' on employers in individual contracts, to establish and maintain some rather substantial 'claims' to social benefits from the state, and enforces contractual agreements, whilst the parties are left free to use their 'liberties' to bargain over the initial terms and conditions of the agreements.

In the post-war period, these arrangements were augmented and, indeed, maintained by the state's further use of its power in a number of ways. First, in accordance with the Rehn Model of 1960, it pursued an 'active labour market policy' and so added certain 'claims' to training and other support to the possessory equation. Secondly, through the Co-determination Act of 1976, it acted to allow some moves in the direction of the equalisation of control relations through requiring the joint (capital/labour) regulation of many aspects of the production process. And finally, through the establishment of union-administered, regional Wage Earner Funds, it even allowed labour to encroach upon title by requiring that a percentage of company profits should be transferred to these Funds (Abrahamson and Brostrom, 1980). Despite the minimal results of the last measure, as well as much talk of an endemic economic crisis, an end to unchallenged Social-Democratic political dominance, and accession to the European Community, there has as yet been little movement in the direction of negotiations outside the centralised structure established by the Basic Agreement. Presently, therefore, the Swedish labour law system remains one that is uniquely favourable to the equalisation—if not the dissolution—of capitalist employment relations along not only the dimension of possession, but also along those of control and title.

The evolution of Canadian labour law provides an interesting contrast to that of Sweden in that, as in France, an initially similar post-recognition system based on 'powers' and focused on possessory relations eventually gave way to one based on 'liberties'. Canada remained a colony, but a self-governing one, until 1931, a legal colony for much longer, and shares a very long border and many economic links with the United States. It is therefore not surprising that the development of Canadian labour law shows many signs of both British and American influence. Thus the same variably enforced repressive laws initially governed industrial relations in Canada as in Britain and the United States. However, the transition to a regime of toleration occurred rather differently. Initially, the British model was followed through the passage of legislation in 1872 and 1876, but the protection offered by the Canadian legislation was even more uncertain and its range more restricted. It was more uncertain because it was only available to registered unions and many refused to register, and its range was more restricted because it did not apply to 'public works' of many kinds. Moreover, no equivalent to the 1906 Trades Disputes Act was passed to nullify the legal reasoning that had resulted in the British *Taff Vale* judgment of 1901. Instead, an element of recognition was added to an already hybrid regime of repression and toleration through the passage of a Conciliation Act

(1900) and, more importantly, an Industrial Disputes Investigation Act (IDIA) (1907). These were intended to, and indeed often did, prevent any disruption that might lead to suits for damages by making an appeal to a tripartite tribunal available to any group (that is, not necessarily a unionised one) of 10 or more employees. However, in contrast to the Swedish and French cases, no negotiation, let alone industrial action, was allowed prior to the commencement of conciliatory hearings. Moreover, following the 1919 General Strike in Winnipeg, the limits of legal strike action were still further restricted—and therefore the attractiveness of even such a disadvantageous conciliation system increased—by changes to the provisions relating to sedition in the Criminal Code. Despite a 1925 British Privy Council decision that the IDIA was unconstitutional, which meant that somewhat varying versions of it had to be re-enacted in the individual provinces, this system remained in place until World War II.

The first significant American contribution to the development of Canadian labour thinking came as a result of the triumph at the 1902 Trades and Labor Congress of policies inspired by the American Federation of Labor, concerning the preferability of sole bargaining rights over multi-unionism, and voluntary over compulsory arbitration. Eventually, legislation incorporating these preferences and modelled on the Wagner Act and the Industrial Relations and Disputes Investigation Act (1948) in its federal and state forms, replaced the IDIA and instituted a regime premised on union recognition. The 'liberties' central to this regime, now somewhat more developed as the Labor Code (1970), were later both further entrenched by the presence of indirectly supportive articles in the Charter of Rights and Freedoms (1982) and, more importantly, the restrictions on labour's 'liberties' that they contain or allow have been translated into a far more elaborate array of economic and social claim rights than in the United States. This said, many of the latter 'claims' are currently threatened, and far more grievously than in Sweden or France, by an ongoing process of 'privatisation'. Still, the Canadian labour movement remains far healthier than that of the United States (Weiler, 1983). However, it is interesting to speculate that it might have been still healthier if, contrary to American-inspired trade union verities, the conciliation system had been *underpinned* by strengthened 'liberties', which would have allowed, for example, Swedish-style prior bargaining, instead of being *replaced* by such 'liberties'. Under such circumstances, 'Big Labor' (that is, in the popular mind, sectionalist and striking labour) might not have become such a bugbear, the control might have displaced the possessory dimension as the critical dimension of class relations because of the political sources and institutional density of a regime based on 'powers', and there might therefore have been less likelihood of the disestablishment of so many 'claims' against employers and the state in the employment and welfare areas.

Finally, to end this section I will provide a brief description of Australian developments which, in very general terms, have been structurally similar to those in Canada, except that they exhibit a very different content and temporality. As another former British settler colony, Australia's early labour law reflected British developments very closely in all but two major respects. First, the pace at which British statutes were received varied greatly between the different colonies into which the continent had been divided. Secondly, because of the exigencies created by a generalised labour shortage, the individual labour law represented by Master-Servant Law appears to have been far more salient to the disciplining of labour than collective labour law for most of the 19th century. Thus, although collective labour law followed the same trajectory from repression to toleration as in Britain and Canada, individual employees seldom experienced this as a benefit, since, as in the United States, they continued to suffer the repressiveness of Master-Servant Laws that remained effective and rather widely used until the 1890s. However, despite this unsupportive legal environment and the ravages of the Depression of the 1890s, but largely because of the democratic political environment, unions nevertheless not only established themselves as significant social institutions, but also gained a very significant ally in the form of the Labor Party. With the sometimes-ambivalent support of the unions, the Labor Party put its very considerable political weight behind the proposals for a compulsory arbitration system which were enacted from 1900 onwards. Thus recognition and arbitration came to Australian unions far earlier than in Sweden and in a far more effective form than in Canada. Thus the 'liberties' that labour had demanded were translated into 'powers' at the Australian Commonwealth (later Federal) and state levels which entitled unions, but only unions, to take a gradually broadened array of grievances over pay and conditions to conciliation or arbitration courts, and so make a significant input into the determination of their members' pay and conditions. This system only began to change in the 1990s when the Labor Party, led by Paul Keating, began to dismantle it in the name of a rapprochement with neo-liberalism supposedly made necessary by the competitive pressures attendant on globalisation.

Conclusion

As has been suggested in numerous studies of the development of the welfare state in the 'West', historically capitalism has become socially more vulnerable as it has become more complex in its internal operations and more demanding of its social context. That is, as there has developed an increasing complexity in the tasks of assembling, managing and supervising capital and labour power, as well as realising the commodities that are produced when these elements are combined, capital has become ever more dependent upon the mental labour, loyalty and purchasing power of the embodiments of labour. In this way, then, labour's contribution has had to be recognised, as it has become constitutive of the relations of production and not simply a means of production to be exploited. Put another way, labour's active co-operation, and not just its simple availability, has become a *sine qua non* for the production and realisation of capital. Repression through the use of superior force may ensure the availability of labour, but it is not an effective means of gaining labour's willing co-operation.

In Western Europe, Canada and Australia, an alternative to force was found within the legal sphere—through the translation of 'liberties', whether extant or demanded, in the realms of association, bargaining or industrial action, into economic and social claims on, or powers vis à vis, companies and/or the state. That this occurred was thanks largely to the co-presence alongside a capitalist economy of more or less liberal-democratic political, ideological and legal formations. In different nation states one or other of these formations was often more important than the others, as indeed were the changes brought about by wars, but in all of them the net result was the emergence of a substantial segment of the population positioned by the working class and constituted by some form or other of socialist ideology and with some access to political power. In the United States, too, a full panoply of similarly liberalistic institutions co-existed with a capitalist economy. However, for reasons that have long fascinated historians and social scientists, the discourse that constituted the American capitalist class was an especially aggressive form of individualism, whilst that which constituted the working class was not socialist. The net result was that when labour eventually achieved some access to political power in the course of the New Deal of the 1930s, the translation of civil into economic and social rights was minimal as compared to what was achieved elsewhere amongst the early industrialisers. What is more, no such translation occurred when labour's liberties were subsequently restricted. Unsurprisingly, therefore, violence remained (Adamic, 1963), and indeed remains, far more characteristic of American industrial disputes than is the case elsewhere—a seldom commented upon consequence of the 'all or nothing' character of disputes where labour has recourse to little more than an attenuated set of 'liberties'.

Notes

1 The present and much of the following chapter was first written as a comparative sociological commentary on a series of studies commissioned by the International Institute of Social History (Amsterdam) and selected by Marcel van der Linden of the Institute and Richard Price of the Department of History, University of Maryland (van der Linden and Price, 1999). The other participants and the titles of the papers upon which much of what follows depends were as follows:
Adelman, J, 'Labour law in 20th century Argentina', Department of History, Princeton University.
Fransson, S, 'Freedom of contract, parity and collective regulation: an essay on the historical development of collective labour law in Sweden, 1734–1995', Department of Law, Gothenburg University.
Garon, S, 'Collective labor law in Japan since 1882', Department of History, Princeton University.
Gibson, D, 'Collective labour law in Canada, 1812–1982: The branch plant has a few ideas of its own', Department of Law, Alberta.
Hall, M, 'Labor and the law in Brazil', Department of History, Campinas

University, Sao Paulo.
Olszak, N, 'The historical development of collective labour law: France', Robert Schuman University, Strasbourg.
Markey, R, 'The development of collective labour law in Australia, 1788–1914', Wollongong University.
Rubin, G, 'The historical development of collective labour law: the United Kingdom', Department of History, University of Kent.
Shieh, G-S, 'Cultivation, control and dissolution: the historical transformation of the Labor Union Act of Taiwan, 1911–1990', Institute of Sociology, Academia Sinica, Taiwan.
Stone, K, 'Labor and the American State: the evolution of labor law in the United States', Department of Law, Cornell University.
Woodiwiss, A, 'Colonialism and the development of labour law in Hong Kong'. Another and differently focused version appears in Isin and Turner (2002).

2 Both Neumann and Kahn-Freund also refer to a fourth phase of 'incorporation' or 'integration' (Kahn-Freund, 1981, p 30, pp 108–61; and see also Ramm, 1986) where the central institutions in the sphere of industrial relations are participative and include a central role for special labour courts. Although it would be inappropriate to fully justify this conclusion here, I have not sought to discern such a phase in the histories I am considering because I am not convinced that it can be clearly distinguished from that of recognition. Suffice it to say that I do not regard the presence of participative and judicial institutions as necessarily incorporative, let alone fascistic, in their effects, since the wider social significance of the legal 'powers' upon which they rest can vary greatly depending upon which 'liberties' and/or 'claims' they are articulated with as well as on the nature of the social context within which they are embedded—*vide* Sweden.

3 Unless otherwise indicated, more detailed empirical support for the points made below and in the following chapter is contained either in van der Linden and Price (1999), or in my earlier studies of American and Japanese and other Pacific-Asian labour law systems (Woodiwiss, 1990b, 1992, 1998).

Chapter 4
Making human rights work in familialist societies

The appearance of the assertively familialist or—to use the term preferred by its proponents—communitarian discourse of 'Asian Values' has most often been seen as a threat to human rights if not by its proponents then most definitely by many of the discourse's opponents. I do not agree with this perception. On the contrary, it seems to me that, when understood and responded to not politically, but social-scientifically, and with an eye for unintended consequences, the appearance of 'Asian Values' has provided a very necessary challenge to a version of human rights discourse that, had it become hegemonic, would have represented a very considerable threat to the possibility of a truly cosmopolitan world order. The latter, to my mind, would be a world order within which values other than those associated with individualism and liberalism—namely various kinds of communitarianism such as Christian or Social Democracy, and familialisms of various kinds—could continue to command respect and provide guides for both individual and social development.

I have explained at length elsewhere (Woodiwiss, 1998) how I think the challenge posed by 'Asian Values' might be understood and responded to sociologically. That response was long on substantive analysis and stressed the necessity of escaping from essentialist and stereotypical representations of Asian societies. It recommended instead a conception of such societies as varyingly hybridised cousins of, rather than others to, similarly hybridised and varying 'Western' societies. It was, however, rather short on theoretical argumentation, and it is this aspect that I would like to develop in the opening section of this chapter by enriching my earlier argument with borrowings from two additional sources—namely the works of John Rawls and Partha Chatterjee, not as strange a pair of bedfellows as might at first appear, or so I hope to show.

How, then, might reflecting on, to use one of Chatterjee's titles, 'Community in the East' aid us in prising open the human rights box? Essentially, by helping us to realise that, contrary to the conventional wisdom, there is no necessary antipathy between Asian Values or, indeed, any variety of familialism and respect for human rights, since in fact familialist values may be seen to entail respect for human rights provided only that the current, self-appointed and most often liberalistic guardians of the human rights temple can be brought to share this realisation. What, then, are the required circumstances? By what methodology might the guardians be brought to realise this relation?

With a pleasant and encouraging irony, these two questions may be answered together, since the best guides as to the circumstances under which Asian communitarian values may be seen to entail respect for human rights seem to me to have been provided by a number of liberal thinkers. Significantly, though, the thinkers I have in mind—John Rawls, Max Weber and Wesley Hohfeld—all operated at the limits of liberal common sense, since each of them was ultimately prepared to allow the empirical rather than the ideological to be the final judge of theory, with the result that their ideas became usable within other analytical traditions.

Reconciling familialism and human rights

In the present text I am making a very general argument at a global level, and I will therefore largely bracket my appreciation of the actually hybrid character of the societies I will discuss in what follows. Instead I will construct my argument on the basis of a model of what a human rights regime would have to look like to be effective in an ideo-typical familialist society. I will then use this model to provide a standard against which extant, non-Western labour rights regimes may be judged.

In many ways, the most surprising and, given the accusations of betrayal that greeted it, the bravest answer to the question as to how the human rights box might be prised open by considering 'Community in the East' is that produced by the man whom many consider to be the high priest of contemporary liberalism—John Rawls, in his book *The Law of the Peoples* (1999). What caused him to challenge the limits of liberal common sense was a combination of the logic of toleration, the resilient diversity of the global polity, and a very strong sense of the importance of avoiding war. For Rawls, the combined effect of these three elements is to produce a recognition of the possible global legitimacy of a variety of familialism, or what he terms 'decent hierarchical societies'. To be globally legitimate, such a society would have to exhibit the following five characteristics or qualifications to its hierarchical character. First, it should be internationally pacific. Secondly, it should be governed on the basis of a legal system premised upon a minimal set of what Rawls regards as the only truly universalisable human rights: freedom from slavery, liberty of conscience, and the prohibition of genocide. Thirdly, respect for these rights should be enforced by imposing legally enforceable duties or obligations on the population, especially its most powerful members. Fourthly, those who administer such a non-liberal legal system should do so in good faith, in that they are genuinely committed to the underlying familialist values and not simply using them as a fig leaf to hide any kind of self-serving authoritarianism. Fifthly, the polity should include some sort of 'consultative mechanism' that need not be democratic, but which should nevertheless allow genuine communication between the powerful and the less powerful.

Bold and brave though Rawls' suggestion undoubtedly is, in my view it unnecessarily limits the range of truly universalisable human rights and, relatedly, begs at least three questions that require answering if sharing his tolerance is not to result in merely sharing some wishful thinking. These questions are: Why should one expect a rule of law of any kind to be present in the sort of familialist societies he has in mind, let alone a rule of law premised on even a selection of human rights? Why should one expect any mechanism of consultation to be present, let alone one that gives a voice to the less powerful? Finally, can a system of enforcing respect for human rights based on duties and obligations really be regarded as legally equivalent to one based on liberties and freedoms?

As a sociologist rather than a political theorist, Weber subjected the conceptual side of his liberalistically inspired thought to a necessarily more rigorous process of empirical testing than did Rawls. Indeed, induction from observations played an important role in the construction of his ideal types. For this reason, one of Weber's ideal types is of particular pertinence to answering the first two of Rawls' begged questions. This is the ideal type of what Weber calls patriarchalism, or the *ur*-form of what I refer to as familialism. Its pertinence arises because it was induced on the basis of studies of the great familialist ethical systems—namely Judaism, Catholic Christianity, Islam, and Confucianism.

For Weber, patriarchalism was the elementary form of traditional authority, and is defined as follows:

> [It] is the situation where, within a group (household) which is usually organised on both an economic and kinship basis, a particular individual governs who is designated by a definite rule of inheritance. *The decisive characteristic…is the belief of the members that domination, even though it is an inherent traditional right of the master, must definitely be exercized as a joint right in the interests of all members and is thus not freely appropriated by the incumbent.* In order that this shall be maintained, it is crucial that in both cases there is a complete absence of a personal (patrimonial) staff. Hence the master is still largely dependent upon the willingness of the members to comply with his orders since he has no machinery to enforce them. Therefore the members are not yet really subjects (Weber, 1978, p 231, emphasis added).

For Weber, then, patriarchalism was a strictly hierarchical political structure justified by a familialist discourse and resting on an economy and a wider set of social relations structured in large part by kinship. Clearly, given the nature of contemporary state and economic forms, patriarchalism no longer has a political or economic referent outside of some relatively self-subsistent indigenous communities. However, it seems to me that the *belief* which is the 'decisive characteristic' does still have a referent. Patriarchalism today signifies a familialist discourse of rule that, regardless of institutional context, both assumes the naturalness of inequalities in the social relations between people, and justifies these by reference to the respect due to a benevolent father or father-figure or, sometimes, mother-figure, who nonetheless does not 'freely appropriate' all power to himself or herself, but exercises a 'joint right'.

However, for this to be a legitimate discourse of rule today, and given the displacement of kinship relations by the development of the massively powerful elaboration of the idea of a 'personal (patrimonial) staff' represented by the state and the arrival of the capitalist economy, the question that obviously arises is: 'How is the "decisive characteristic", namely the "belief of members that domination...[is]...exercized as a joint right" to be sustained?' Well, the means of sustaining this belief that were discovered, tried and tested in Western Europe in the course of the same displacements of kinship by the rise of the state and capitalism were twofold, and have yet to be improved upon. They were the rule of law, which prevents power being 'freely appropriated by the incumbent', and representative democracy, which ensures that the compliance of the ruled is more or less freely given. In other words, nothing can take the place of the rule of law and of representative democracy, and therefore the rights that underpin them, even in societies that wish to preserve a familialist discourse of rule. And this is why there is no need to restrict the number of truly universalisable human rights in the way that Rawls does.

The answers to the first two of Rawls' begged questions that I therefore derive from Weber are that, given the arrival of the state and capitalism, the rule of law and representative democracy have to be present if familialist regimes are to be regarded as legitimate in their own, let alone Western, terms. Thus whereas Rawls uses the term 'decent' to refer to what he considers to be a legitimate form of Asian familialism, I use the more specific—but within its sphere of pertinence much more demanding—phrase 'enforceable benevolence' (Woodiwiss, 1998, pp 3–4). The latter refers to a mode of governance where, whilst social relations remain distinctly hierarchical, the content of benevolence is democratically decided and its delivery legally and ultimately popularly enforced. The point here is that the social embeddedness of a human rights regime constructed on such a familialist basis should mean that such a regime could prove to be more effective in familialist societies in Asia and elsewhere than one premised on the individualistic or even social-democratic means of qualifying inequality that 'Westerners' have resort to. This is because it would work *with* the grain of the culture rather than against it. And what this means is that subordinates are placed in the position of asking superordinates to live up to their own values rather than, if subordinates were having to insist on their liberties, demanding that they be given something that they had never had and which can be therefore readily branded as an alien cultural intrusion.

I now wish to turn to the issue of how the difference nevertheless represented by all forms of familialism may be accommodated within the discourse of human rights, and therefore to the third of Rawls' begged questions: 'Can a system of enforcing respect for human rights based on duties and obligations really be regarded as legally equivalent to one based on liberties and freedoms?' At this point, the thinker I wish to invoke (again) is

Hohfeld, since what distinguished him from many of today's liberal thinkers was that he paid close attention to the actual language of the constitutional and legal texts within which rights are defined. More specifically, it is his disaggregation of the rights concept that makes it possible to see that duties and obligations in the form of 'powers' and 'claims' ceded may be seen as the equivalents of 'liberties' and freedoms in their social consequences. This, as was explained above (pp 15–16), is also the idea that creates the possibility of translation, and therefore also the possibility of the articulation of social difference within human rights discourse. But why should one think that it is likely to be effective as part of strategy for empowering the weak and the meek? Elsewhere (Woodiwiss, 1998) and in the preceding chapter, I have indicated that evidence for the effectiveness of this analysis may be derived from the historical and contemporary experience of Western Europe. To repeat, with respect to labour rights, only the United States has a labour rights system whose critical premise is a 'liberty', whilst there are not only wholly justiciable, but also, in their contexts, far more effective systems that have been democratically approved and rest on 'liberties' translated into economic and social rights and delivered on the basis of either 'powers' (Australia and France) or 'claims' (Sweden). Thus, reflecting the nature the different forms of rights as diverse means of achieving overlapping ends, the process of translation I am arguing for is already well established politically and juridically with respect to labour rights. Moreover, despite their often constitutionally guaranteed freedom of association, unions have often felt able to accept qualifications to their independence. These include the virtually universal requirement that they should register with a state agency, which is typically empowered both to require that their constitutions contain certain basic elements, and to exercise an oversight over their internal affairs and so ensure that the constitution is observed, as well as the many laws that restrict the organisational, tactical and even strategic and political options available to unions. In other words, even Western unions have accepted many qualifications to their independence vis à vis the state. They have also, in some instances and more controversially, accepted qualifications to their independence from employers. Here I am thinking of the many types of joint consultation arrangements, as exemplified by many Western European cases as well as the Australian one.

What, of course, has allowed trade unions to accept these qualifications to their independence and, indeed, freedom of association is not only the confidence imparted by participation in a wider set of democratic institutions, but also the fact that these qualifications have had a positive side in the form of some bargained compensation for this acceptance. Typically, this compensation has taken the translated form of legally enforceable 'powers' or 'claims', including a wide array of statutory contractual terms plus welfare entitlements of many and various kinds. As will be explained below, very similar developments have occurred in Pacific Asia, but only where representative democracy and/or the rule of law have been present. Equally significantly, such developments have not occurred in my two Latin

American cases, where neither condition has yet been met for any sustained period of time.

Before outlining the separate histories of the occurrence and non-occurrence of such translations, I will provide an abstract answer to the question concerning the effectiveness of such translation as a means of empowerment by deploying an argument I have derived from Chatterjee's (1998) work. Although what I shall take from Chatterjee's work is abstract, I should point out that his original argument was also empirically produced: it arose out of his still ongoing radical rethinking of the history of the 'modern state' in India. The central point made in the course of this rethinking was that, as in the West but probably to an even greater degree, neither the colonial state nor its post-colonial successor has ruled in the way that liberal political theory suggested that it should—that is, by recognising individuals as sovereign powers and therefore the creators of a civil society which ultimately controls the state and with which the state has to deal as the ultimate source of sovereignty. Instead, Chatterjee reworks the insights summarised in Gramsci's concept of 'hegemony', and also contained in Michel Foucault's reflections on liberal governance and the concept of 'governmentality' (Burchell *et al*, 1991), to argue that the state has actually ruled on the basis of its own presumed sovereignty. And it has done so in India not by constituting individuals as autonomous subjects, as in the West, but by constituting them as members of what are often termed 'communities'—such as castes, tribes or ethnic groups, for its own governmental purposes, whether these be matters of economics, public order, health, education or whatever.

His point is not so much that state discourse about communities is phoney, although it often is—but that, phoney or not, it is how the state actually relates to its citizens, and therefore represents, wholly unintentionally, the provision of a means through which the population may in time be able to transform itself into a new form of sovereign citizenry. That is, the way to democratise the state and civilise capital is not so much through painstakingly trying to create a civil society that might anyway be illusory, but, instead, for individuals and groups to return the interest and attention of the state wherever and whenever it takes an interest in them. This is a thought that clearly has wide and counter-intuitive implications for the West too, in that (contra much Western communitarian theory—for example, Puttnam, 2000) it suggests that the alleged decline in the vibrancy of civil society is more likely to be caused by the social *retreat* of the state rather than its activism. Obviously enough, the more immediate point I wish to take from all this is that where, as in much of Asia and the South more generally, governmentalities produce civil societies rather than vice versa, not only are states, almost by definition, better able to cede 'claims' and 'powers' than respect 'liberties' and 'immunities', but also when pressured they can actually deliver, as the post-war histories of Japan, Hong Kong and Singapore all attest (see below). Thus the answer to the question as to why one might think that making the two human rights covenants translatable into each other's terms could provide an effective means of protecting the weak and the meek is that this is what is suggested by both the *modus operandi* and the histories of both Western European and post-colonial states.

In sum, my suggestion is that the lesson to be learnt from reflecting on 'Community in the East' is not that the current privileging of civil and political over economic and social rights should be reversed, but, rather, that valued aspects of familialist difference and, indeed, of what might be called 'strong communitarian' approaches more generally, may be preserved by allowing the mutual translatability of the two covenants. The principal advantage of embracing the idea of translation, then, is that it provides an internationally legitimate means with which to reconcile cultural differences.

Late industrialisation, familialism and the development of labour rights

In order to differentiate my position from the Liberal and Modernisationist argument that respect for human rights is a natural consequence of capitalist development, I wish to begin this section by insisting that history makes it clear that there is nothing automatic about the realisation of such self-civilising on the part of capital. No history makes this clearer than Japan's. Neither liberal-democratic nor even liberal legal institutions were part of capitalism's social context as it emerged in Japan, and partially as a consequence of this the working class as a whole was neither constituted by socialist discourse nor had access to political power (Woodiwiss, 1992). Thus, despite that fact that complex forms of capital were present in pre-war Japan, the need for labour's active co-operation was met by mobilising paternalistic political and ideological forces that constituted the working-class population as loyal servants of the Emperor, and to the benefit of capital and the embodiments of patriarchal power more generally. Thanks to Japan's defeat in World War II and the particular character of the reforms forced upon it by the American-led Occupation, hybrid liberal/familialist formations became constitutive of Japanese society and its classes, with the result that a fortunate and quite large minority of the working-class population ultimately became the beneficiaries of a limited form of 'enforceable benevolence'.

As Sheldon Garon (1999) has correctly argued, to suggest, as I did in an earlier contribution (Woodiwiss, 1992, Chapter 2), that the history of Japanese labour law does not include a phase of 'toleration' in the Neumann/Kahn-Freund sense somewhat overstates the difference between that history and its 'Western' equivalents. For two reasons I came to see this more clearly in the context of the collaborative project upon which this chapter draws. The first was the inclusion of France, Sweden and Canada, with their phases of combined repression and toleration, amongst the array of comparators. The second was the fact that in all four cases the elements of 'toleration' were present as a result of the changing disposition of state power, albeit differently enacted. This is significant because until the 1920s, Japanese law as applied to labour was undoubtedly and simply repressive. An emergent capital sponsored and supported by a centralised and undemocratic paternalist state was unquestionably dominant across all the subsets of class relations. Only a tiny section of skilled workers in the newest industries had any freedom to bargain over their individual terms of employment. Even the French Civil Code was considered potentially too permissive, with the result that the Prussian alternative was preferred since it maintained a place for paternalist structures and relationships alongside liberalistic ones. Moreover, during the 1920s, the period of so-called Taisho Democracy—and despite the emergence of a surprisingly resilient and, in comparative terms, not especially small labour movement—there was little substantive change even though there were some ostensibly significant legal changes, most importantly the passage of the Canadian-inspired Conciliation Law of 1926. Nonetheless, the judgment that little changed remains a point of difference between Garon and myself. He stresses the significance of the selective enforcement of the Police or Peace Preservation Law and, presumably, the few years when resort to conciliation was voluntary, whilst I stress the rapid rise of the involuntary, police-administered 'sabre mediation' that Garon himself (1987, pp 199ff) has described so well (Woodiwiss, 1992, pp 64–65). In other words, Garon stresses the brief emergence of a regime of toleration based on the delegation to private parties of certain state 'powers', whilst I stress the rapid *withdrawal* of these same 'powers' by the state and their subsequent administration by the state's repressive apparatus rather than, say, the judiciary. For all that, we are both agreed that the early 1930s saw the return of repression, qualified only by the grant to unions of the very doubtful 'powers' associated with them becoming organs of the state.

As Garon has also shown, the law that initiated the post-war 'recognition' phase and represents the core of the present Japanese labour law system—the Trade Union Law of 1949—owed as much, if not more, to a draft prepared by the Japanese Home Ministry's Social Bureau in 1925 than to the American Wagner Act, as most previous writers on the topic have argued. In my view, the most striking consequence of this continuity between the pre- and post-war Japanese legislation which extends to the other labour laws that have defined the post-war Japanese system, notably the Labour Standards Law and Labour Relations Adjustment Law, is the significance retained by conciliatory institutions within the industrial relations system. Thus, as in Sweden, and although the Japanese system also rests on the granting to labour of certain unambiguously specified 'liberties', it has become in operation a system based on labour's possession of 'powers' and 'claims' justified on a familialist basis: above all, the 'power' to require representation on the panels of the Labour Commissions that are the instruments of conciliation, as well as to refer disputes to such commissions, and the 'claim' on companies to lifetime employment. When combined with the broader social continuities between pre- and post-war Japan, as well as the court system's preference for conciliation over adjudication, the net result has been the restoration of a transformed and very un-Swedish familialism to Japanese labour law in the form of what I and others have termed *'kigyoshugi'* (the enterprise as family) (Woodiwiss, 1992, Chapter 5).

The post-war entry of *kigyoshugi* into labour law has transformed the conception of the employment relationship in the private sector that was basic to both the New Constitution (1947) and the 1949 Trade Union Law. In other words, the post-war American-inspired recognition of the different interests of capital and labour that was fundamental to the legislation of that period has been ever more confidently *denied* as the social and judicial commitment to the limited and hierarchical communitarianism of the company bespoken by *kigyoshugi* has grown. In another surprising and fascinating instance of transnationally inspired hybridity, it seems that, alongside *kigyoshugi*, arguments drawn from the Weimar Republic's social-democratic labour law by lawyers acting for post-war Japanese unions played a significant role in helping the Japanese judiciary produce the doctrine of lifetime employment that is the best known sign of this commitment (Kettler and Tackney, 1997). In Hohfeld's terms, then, the period since 1949 has seen a striking reduction in the 'liberties' of Japanese employees and unions as the control dimension of the property relation has become ever more salient within large companies. The same period has also seen these liberties translated into not only an increase in 'powers' (to participate in joint consultation fora, for example), but also into very substantial increases in 'claims' to such as company welfare benefits and, most importantly, to an apparently irreversible claim to 'lifetime employment'—all justified on a familialist basis.

Restricted though the numbers of people concretely, as opposed to nominally, benefiting from these translated incidents of liberty may be, it is nevertheless important to acknowledge that, thanks to the demand for consistency inherent in legal discourse under conditions of judicial independence, successful, but as yet not fully tested, efforts have been made to extend the legal entitlement to 'lifetime employment' beyond the confines of the large-scale corporate sector (Schregle, 1993; Sugeno, 1992, pp 65, 156). Thus, in the absence of a written contract (the normal state of affairs in Japan), the courts will generally find an implied promise to provide lifetime employment no matter what the size of the company. Moreover, the wider legal, social-structural and cultural supports that this doctrine possesses have thus far proved robust enough to sustain it through a prolonged recession and the continuing 'hollowing out' of the economy as production has been relocated to other, and sometimes lower-waged, countries. Of course, many companies have sought either to reduce their exposure to the doctrine's consequences by taking on far fewer 'regular' employees, or by offering inducements (not all of them pleasant: Salgardo, 1999) to take early retirement. However, that such measures have been adopted itself suggests both the legal strength of the position of young and mid-career regular employees, and the wider ideological value of 'lifetime employment'.

In sum, these developments in Japanese labour law illustrate how the obligations inherent in the familialist (in this case Confucian) concept of 'benevolence' may be made legally enforceable, and thus instance a neo-familialism—'neo' because the family has been displaced by the company as the carrier of the discourse. In Japan, this has resulted from established bargained norms, like lifetime employment, being read by the courts as implied contractual terms. In the light of the broadly similar cultural environment in other familialist societies, there is therefore every reason to think that a similar result could by achieved in other such societies by legislatively specifying the 'powers' to participate in decision-making and 'claims' (to training, security of employment, and/or social programmes, for example), into which 'liberties' and/or 'immunities' must be translated if they are to be restricted.

However, to be successful, any attempt to inscribe the discourse of rights within familialism has both to be rigorously enforced at the margins, preferably by unions as well as by the state, and therefore to involve the maintenance of certain irreducible 'liberties' as well as labour access to political power. Here again, a critical lesson may be learnt from the Japanese case—a lesson that has indeed recently been instructive in South Korea (Lee, 1998). In my view, the most important of these 'liberties' and 'immunities' are those that protect the freedom of ordinary employees to withhold their consent without having to resign. In other words, where one has enterprise or 'in-house' unions, as in Japan, it is essential not simply that labour rights are fundamentally employee rather than union rights, but also that, again as in Japan (Woodiwiss, 1992, pp 142–4), they are continuously exercisable, not only vis à vis employers but also vis à vis incumbent unions through employees exercising a 'liberty' to create a second union or to sustain an already existing 'minority' union. In other words, from labour's standpoint, and contrary to 'Western' labour's experience, the possibility of multi-unionism should be seen in a positive rather than in a negative light—that is, where the efficacy of the rights represented by American-style employer 'unfair labour practice' provisions is reduced, as they invariably are where there are participative structures and/or enterprise unions, it is important that this be balanced by a strengthening or a broadening of a positive right to self-organisation on the part of all employees in order to prevent the suborning of unions (see also Leader, 1992, Chapter 10).

Post-colonial industrialisation, familialism and labour rights

In contrast to Japan, in each of the cases considered below, save Taiwan, one liberal institution at least was co-present with capitalism from the beginning of their modern histories—namely an imported, individualistically based legal system. Thus, even whilst they remained colonies, there were in each of the territories at least formal limits to the state's power vis à vis individuals, especially property holders, and capital's power vis à vis individual labourers. In law, the state had to respect individual property rights and the privity of contractual relations. Additionally, the holders of property rights had to respect labourers' rights in contract and tort, minimal though these rights were. There was also a formally independent, though often racist, judiciary required to decide the disputes that were brought before it on a consistent basis, and as determined by an evolving body of doctrine whose content was significantly determined by case law and statutory developments in the pertinent colonial or former colonial power. That is, to varying degrees, colonial legal systems were in receipt of laws produced within metropolitan jurisdictions where the civilising of capital was far more advanced than locally, even though colonial legal systems were simultaneously destructive of indigenous laws and social relations. Finally, the presence of the rule of law meant that there also existed modes of enforcing the rights so imported—that is, by bringing cases to court, seeking injunctions, obtaining damages, and meting out fines or prison sentences. Of course, there were marked asymmetries in access to these means of enforcement and in the distribution of rights as between capital and labour. This was because of both the continuing inequalities in the pertinent metropolitan countries, and the much slower pace at which improvements in labour's rights, as compared to developments in capital's property and contractual rights, were received by the colonies and former colonies. There were also great differences in the levels of enforcement that the rights of capital and labour attracted or were able to avail themselves of, thanks to racism as well as economic inequalities and differences. Nevertheless, an individualistic variant of the rule of law did become a constitutive part of the disciplinary structures of all but one of the social formations discussed below, which is a significant difference from the Japanese case.

Notwithstanding the racism that informed colonial, and indeed most instances of post-colonial, governance, what makes the presence of an individualistic legal system a difference of particular significance is the fact that, in all these territories except for Taiwan, imported capitalism and the rule of law therefore co-existed in some tension with indigenous familialist political and ideological structures. In Japan, this tension was far less marked because the rule of law as promulgated in the initial 19th century Civil and Commercial Codes continued the privilege traditionally accorded to certain familialist elements (Woodiwiss, 1992, pp 51–58). However, again in all but Taiwan, as both capital and the state were localised, respect for—or at least acceptance of—the possibility that individual or, indeed, labour rights might come into conflict with patriarchally-defined obligations also became constitutive of the colonies concerned as they moved towards independence or, in Hong Kong's case, towards restoration to China. In sum, an individualistic and atomistic conception of rights became embedded in these territories precisely because they had been colonies rather than independent states like Japan; that is, because such a conception was necessary to secure the colonists' property rights against the threat abstractly, if seldom practically, posed by the indigenous patriarchal powers. Thus, in a structural sense if no other, capitalism was a rather less ambiguous ally of rights discourse in the colonies than it was in the metropolitan countries in advance of the emergence of the social-structural support potentially provided by more developed forms of capitalism.

For these reasons, then, despite the frequent absence of democracy the issue as to whether or not rights are respected has long been an issue within the societies to be discussed in a way in which it was not in pre-war Japan. Indeed, anger at the hypocrisy of the colonial powers as they spoke of rights amongst peoples whose rights they were at the same moment neglecting or violating did much to fuel demands for independence, as well as to provide language with which they might be expressed. Thus rights became part, indeed a priviledge part, of the constitutions of all but one of the terroteries discussed here when they became independent or, in Hong Kong's case, as it was belatedly prepared for reversion of Chinese sovereignty. That is, rights occupy an important role in such constitutional texts not just becausethe presence of some rights is now expected as part of the price of admission to the 'modern' or 'civilised' capitalist world, but also because a rights presence also represents a claim to self-respect as well as, sometimes, to moral superiority vis à vis former colonial masters. That said, once freedom from colonial tutelage had been achieved, it then transpired that the social support for rights discourse provided by the colonial state and its capitalist clients, albeit very often in the breach, then virtually disappeared. Thereafter, a new balance had to be struck between the content of rights discourse and the duties now more assertively projected by the famialist discourses proclaimed by the new states and emergent national capitals as they formulated their 'state projects' (Jessop, 1990).

Each of present sample of societies that havehad their most intensive experience of industrialisation in the post-1945 period may be charaterised as broadly famialist,albeit with a Catholic rather than Confucian inflection in the sake of brazil and Argentina. Thus, it is not surprising that there are some striking similarities with Japan in the ways that their labour law system have evolved. However, there are also some striking differences where, as in all of my cases save Taiwan, there has been greater openness to Western influnces.

In Brazil during the first third of the 20th century, elements of repression and toleration co-existed within the labour law system. A sometimes-unused repressive police power was combined with seldom-enforced protective 'claims' with respect to vulnerable workers. Under the Vargas regime, unions with self bargaining rigths were legally recoginsed provided they fulfilled certain regorous registeration criteria. On this basis, the 'liberties' unions had been demanding were translated into the 'powers' associated with the right of representation on the benches of the tripartite Labour Court, which decided industrial relations cases and certain 'claims' on employers and the state with respect to holidays and pensions, as well as access to the Labour Courts. When the Vargas regime reconsructed itself on Italian fascist principles in 1937, the Labour Courts remains but strikes were totally forbidden. The right to strike was, however, translated into 'powers' that followed from their becoming agents of political representation, and so recipients of a substantial share of the receipts of a state-imposed 'union tax' out of which unions were expected to meet various welfare 'claims' from their members and, in 1939, a minimum wage law.

Despite Vargas' fall in 1945, little has changed formally since then, although there have been significant changes in the way the system has been applied, depending on the political complexion of the government. Many of the strikes that eventually forced a very marked liberalisation of the system's application in the 1980s, especially with respect to union autonomy, were organised outside of the 'official' unions because employees were dissatisfied with how the unions were using their 'powers', and perhaps especially their use of the union tax with respect to meet and/or enforce employee 'claims'.

Argentina's labour law system has also been indelibly marked by the familialist context within which it emerged. This context meant that political or control relations rapidly gained pre-eminence amongst the ensemble of class relations as the society developed, with the result that the executive apparatuses of the state quickly became the principal location of state power and therefore the object of political interest. In contrast to the Japanese and Brazilian cases, but because of the relatively greater strength of the labour movement, by 1920 labour's private bargaining had gained the surprisingly positive support of a state executive, which refused to deploy its repressive powers and instead provided sympathetic mediation and issued decrees favouring the labour interest. However, these gains were not translated into either 'liberties', 'powers' or 'claims' and proved to be very short-lived, with the result that a brief period of toleration rapidly gave way to a prolonged one of repression.

Recognition occurred only after a revived trade union movement had again succeeded in forging an alliance with elements of the executive, arising out of mutual need. In 1946, the incoming Peronist government granted registered, and therefore state-approved, unions a combination of benefits (American-style sole bargaining rights and conditional support from the Labor Secretariat), specific 'liberties' (organising and bargaining rights) and some vaguer participative 'powers'. This system was legally formalised in 1953, but by then its dependence on state-sponsorship had become clear, with the result that it became increasingly difficult for unions to exercise their 'liberties', and their 'powers' disappeared once they refused to become unquestioning clients of the executive. Succeeding periods of Peronist dictatorship, military repression, liberalisation, military repression, the restoration of Peronism, military repression and, beginning in 1983, liberalisation again have left the system remarkably unchanged formally. Instead, it has simply been in varying states and degrees of suspension. Ironically, and tragically—in institutional if not industrial terms—the unions have tended to do best during periods of repression when they have become the repositories of oppositional sentiment. The result is that their leaders have tended to become self-interested political brokers rather than effective economic negotiators, able to block the construction of a new system but unable to restore the old one.

Turning to Taiwan, the most striking characteristic of the social context within which labour law has evolved is its triply familialist character—that is,

Taiwan's indigenous culture is familialist, as was that of Japanese colonial government, and as is that brought from China in 1949. During the colonial period, unions enjoyed not even the brief period of administrative and legislative toleration extended to Japanese unions. Because of the political, and indeed military as well as social, context within which it was developed, the labour law that the Kuomintang brought to Taiwan in 1949 was even more consciously political in character than any of the other hybrid repressive/ tolerant systems outlined in this section. The union movement as well as the labour law system was imported lock, stock and officials from China along with the rest of a thoroughly corporatist state structure, and embedded with the help of a grant of a little more autonomy and ferocious state repression of any indigenous resistance. In line with a Chinese law of 1943, both registration and, in the sectors where they existed, membership of unions with sole bargaining rights were compulsory, strikes were forbidden and collective agreements had to be approved by government. Thus the Taiwanese labour law system was one of minimal 'liberties' to bargain and 'powers' to seek state-approval for the results of bargaining. Little has changed since, save for the gradual 'Taiwanisation' of union staffs and the permitting of Japanese-inspired 'plant' or enterprise unions.

However, in response to the rise of a separatist Taiwanese nationalist movement in the 1980s, which in part took the form of the rise of an unofficial union movement, some radical proposals for the reform of the Labor Union Act were made in 1990. These suggest that the state's political security is still the paramount concern rather than liberalisation, let alone the establishment of an autonomous union movement. Thus, first, it was proposed that trade union membership should no longer be compulsory, strikes should be legal (with notice), and union competition should be allowed at plant level. But, secondly, it was also proposed that unions should be reorganised on an enterprise basis and that state officials should attend union meetings and approve any bargaining agreement. Although there are clear signs of learning from Japan' in these proposals with respect to the enterprise as the unit of organisation and the permitting of dual unionism (Liou, 1993), the closeness of the system of state control and the absence of any clearly enforceable contractual or social 'claims' on either capital or the state mean that nothing is envisaged comparable to the Japanese translations.

In Hong Kong, surprisingly, and refusing all speculation on what might happen in the future now that it has reverted to Chinese sovereignty, a system closer to 'enforceable benevolence', if rather different to the Japanese model, appears to have emerged. But 'surprisingly' only if one forgets that what underpins the Japanese system and distinguishes it most sharply from those in Brazil, Argentina and Taiwan is not so much a familialist set of values, but the latter's symbiosis with the rule of law and articulation with political democracy and the possibility of dual unionism. Despite its non-democratic colonial form, the limitations on executive fiat and the intrusion on private arrangements that the rule of law represents appear to have incubated a labour law system in Hong Kong that approaches one of 'enforceable benevolence'.

That is, one in which, after a long period of combined repression and toleration, post-recognition 'liberties' have been non-trivially translated into enforceable and almost universal individual contractual, as well as reasonably widespread social, 'claims'. Significantly in terms of the present argument, these 'claims' far exceed, in terms of the benefits they provide, any that were gained when unions had only their 'liberties' to depend upon. Additionally, the enforceability of such 'claims' is reinforced by the possibility, if seldom the actuality, of a union pluralism in the workplace to complement that which exists at the confederational level. This said, and despite the entrenched nature of the rule of law, the huge weakness of labour law in Hong Kong is the continuing absence of political democracy, and therefore the ease with which it may degenerate in the direction of a restrictive paternalism.

The society that, again surprisingly to some reviewers of my earlier book (Woodiwiss, 1998), is structurally closest to representing a realised instance of 'enforceable benevolence' is Singapore. After 1946, and as in Hong Kong, the hybrid repressive/tolerant regime of the colonial authorities gradually gave way to recognition based upon British-style 'immunities'. Domestic self-government came in 1958, independence in 1963, and Britain finally gave up even its military base in 1967. In the context of a very small and underdeveloped private capitalist sector, and such rapidly dwindling colonial interest, the balance with respect to control or political relations was clearly the most salient to the determination of the overall balance of class relations. Thus the People's Action Party (PAP) was the key player in determining the nature of this balance. In the event, the PAP systematically diminished labour's 'liberties' so as to shift the possessory and control balances to the advantage of the multinational, local and state-owned enterprises that it wished to attract to and/or encourage in Singapore.

However, both because of its social-democratic ideology and the fact that labour was almost the nation's only resource, the PAP compensated labour for the decline in its 'liberties' by translating them into the 'powers' represented by the corporatist structure created by the 'symbiosis' between the party and the National Trade Union Congress in 1965, and the contractual and social 'claims' represented by the Employment Act (1968) and the government's numerous social programmes. The significance of the latter is that they have delivered citizenship rights to good quality public housing, educational opportunities and the economic security achieved through the Central Provident Fund (a compulsory savings scheme to which employers as well as employees contribute). The extent of these translations is far in excess of those delivered in Hong Kong and, more importantly, far in excess of what it is plausible to imagine employees could have achieved through the deployment of their former 'liberties'. What is more, given the existence of both political democracy and the rule of law, it would seem that the PAP has been an instrument for the exercise of a 'joint right' and therefore acting as a good patriarch. However, strong doubts may legitimately be raised about the independence of the judiciary and political freedom in a society where even Supreme Court Justices are subject to a period of probation and government ministers threaten 'disloyal' voters with discriminatory cuts in their social benefits. Moreover, and critically, it is also clear that there is a limit to the extent that the state's benevolence is enforceable and that the state itself defines this limit by the strict control it exercises over union and NGO formation and activity. That is, what undermines any claim that Singapore might represent an achieved instance rather than simply a pointer towards a new model of labour rights is the fact that there is no legal way for labour to reactivate its right to freedom of association.

Conclusion

As I have pointed out elsewhere (Woodiwiss, 1998, pp 50–51), the context within which we now have to think about labour rights is not only one marked by globalisation, but also by a shift from possessory to control relations as the critical dimension of employment relations (see above, p 20). In order to bring out the significance of these changes, I would like to specify the national and transnational context-dependency of the effectiveness of the various modalities of legal intervention in the capital/labour relation by comparing two polar cases and drawing a general conclusion from the preceding analysis. In a 'Northern' economy (like that of the United States in the 1950s) composed primarily of medium-sized and/or first-generation corporate capitals operating at the heads of commodity chains within a protected market and producing goods for which there is strong demand, a traditional labour law system configured in terms of 'liberties' and focused on possessory relations may be sufficient to allow labour to secure some redress of the inequalities that are intrinsic to capitalist relations of production. Under such circumstances, an employer possesses some autonomy and labour is free to attempt to take advantage of this. However, in a strongly dualistic 'Southern' economy (like that of Brazil today), wherein a large number of petty commodity producers and small capitals are organised by a small number of large capitals (many of which are transnationals) operating within an 'open' global market at the lowest level of the commodity chain, a traditional labour law system configured in terms of 'liberties' is most unlikely to be adequate to secure labour's ability to seek a redressing of the imbalances in the employment relation. This is because, although possessory relations may continue to be the most salient of the elements within the property relation to local capitals as such, the wider economic context, and especially local capital's subordination to transnational capital, means that the control relations that are most salient to transnational capital take effective precedence in the governance of the small enterprises, and so render moot the effects of a labour law system based on 'liberties'. In sum, under the latter circumstances employers often possess very little autonomy and so it is often beside the point that labour has the liberty to attempt to force them to exercise any minimal autonomy they have to labour's benefit. As in the case of Japanese main contractor/sub-contractor relations, if the exercise of such a liberty interrupts production, the corporation at the head of the commodity chain will simply increase its orders to other suppliers, or seek new ones.

Thus the necessity of conceptual translation arises for two reasons. First, the recognition that there are different ways of writing or designing rights which are capable of having equivalent outcomes. To repeat, only the United States has a labour rights system whose critical premise is a 'liberty', whilst there are not only wholly justiciable, but also, in their contexts, far more effective systems that have been democratically approved and have as their critical premises either 'powers' (Australia and France) or 'claims' (Japan and Sweden). It also makes clear, therefore, that, whilst the major failings of the less effective or otherwise flawed systems relate to limitations on freedom of association, this does not necessarily mean that they should be reconstructed on American lines, but most likely that the existing 'claims' and 'powers'—that is, economic and social rights—should be more effectively articulated with this 'liberty'. Secondly, whilst writing rights with a stress on freedom of association as 'liberties' or 'immunities' may well mean that they pass the current variant of the justiciability test, it also means that they are unlikely to be effective as a means of achieving the desired outcome, as indeed the currently parlous state of labour protection in the United States would also suggest (Human Rights Watch, 2000).

What the Japanese, Hong Kong and Singaporean experiences suggest, then, is that, because of the whole South's and not just Pacific Asia's shared familialism, any southern unions seeking the translation of their 'liberties' or 'immunities' into enforceable 'claims' on their employers' and/or the states' benevolence should find the courts and, indeed, governments on their side, provided of course that governments abstain from repressive legislation and that the rule of law exists. This is because the syllogism that has come to dominate Japanese labour law, and which was produced by the social-structural entity that comprises familialist social relations, should gradually appear within other jurisdictions too. This syllogism is as follows: if the loyalty that the employee owes to the company justifies restrictions on employee 'liberties' with respect to industrial action, and results in improved economic performance, then the companies that benefit from this loyalty must fulfil the expectations of those who have placed their trust in them and provide labour with economic security.

The strategic political proposition that the Japanese experience prompts, therefore, is that the labour rights system that stands the best chance of being enforced in the largely familialist South is one that is written in such a way that: (1) it mobilises the familialist cultural and social-structural biases, so to speak, of a particular locale in its favour; and (2) it is pertinent to the forms of the property relation obtaining amongst the capitals it seeks to regulate. Thus, whereas it may make sense to suggest that the solution for labour's woes in the United States may begin with the enhancement of labour's right to free speech (Human Rights Watch, 2000), this is most unlikely to be the case elsewhere. In the cases of Brazil, Argentina and Taiwan, for example, it does not seem appropriate that 'liberties' should be sought for their own sake since, as in Hong Kong during the 1950s, their granting may simply result in unions being free to fail, either because the mass of the labour force is unorganisable or because of multiple pre-emptive measures now undertaken by, or available to, the multinationals and their sub-contractors (Woodiwiss, 1998, pp 78–79). Rather, contrary to one of the leading tenets of Western trade union wisdom, the pursuit of 'liberties' should focus on allowing the possibility of multi-unionism, since this provides a structural impediment to corruption in that it may prevent union leaders from becoming creatures of either the state or the corporations, and should be pursued as part of a strategy wherein the aim is the enhancement and juridification of 'powers' and 'claims' that have often been granted in the past but seldom enforced, as the tragic case of the Philippines graphically attests (Woodiwiss, 1998, Chapter 3). This is because not only will they then be able to 'call' the moral bluff of those who claim familial authority, but they will also be in a position to exert pressure on state institutions that should be better able than they to discipline rogue employers, whether they are locals or multinationals.

There is at least one immediately obvious problem with the strategy I have proposed. This is the danger that translation could also be the occasion for regression. I should, then, say something about how I think this danger could be avoided by elaborating a little on the procedural aspect of the translation work that I advocate. As I presently conceive it, translation would be a formal procedure additional but akin to the current arrangements pertaining to treaty reservations (Lijnzaad, 1995). That is, as part of the reporting process, a formal, public and reasoned notification of an intention to translate one or other of labour's 'liberties' into pertinent economic and social rights would have to be lodged with the pertinent UN committee, which would assess and comment upon it in the light of both its own understandings of what the relevant treaty requires, and those set before it by other expert and interested parties. As a result, not only would the international community know what was at stake, and so be able to decide whether or not to accept the translation, but so too would the population of the state party making the notification who should, of course, be able to make a political issue of it if they wish. In this way, then, the possibility of regression should be obviated, although the result might often be an agreement to disagree, the refusal of the UN to sanction a particular translation, and severe doubts about whether or not a particular treaty article was being enforced. However, the resulting aporia and doubts are inevitable given the intrinsic difficulties of the human rights project, and the great advantage over the present situation would be that the problems the project faces would be made visible as opposed to remaining the liminal sources of distrust they are currently.

As I will argue in the following chapter, pursuit of the strategy proposed here also suggests that there may yet be a way out of the current stalemate on the Social Clause at the WTO, and therefore there may eventually come a day when employment relations might become globally justiciable, like property and contractual relations, and when multinational and transnational corporations are no longer able to play Southern and Northern labour off against one another. Such a momentous development could only occur if not only the countries of the West rediscovered the pertinence of the familialist dimensions of their own histories, but also the countries of the South finally found the confidence to learn from themselves as well as from the North.

Chapter 5
Justiciability and the need for cosmopolitan 'core' labour standards

> Whereas universal and lasting peace can be established only if it is based upon social justice;
>
> And whereas conditions of labour exist involving such injustice, hardship and privation to large numbers of people as to produce unrest so great that the peace and harmony of the world are imperilled; and an improvement in those conditions is urgently required; as, for example, by the regulation of the hours of work, including the establishment of the maximum working day and week, the regulation of the labour supply, the prevention of unemployment, the provision of an adequate living wage, the protection of the worker against sickness, disease and injury arising out of his employment, the protection of children, young persons and women, provision for old age and injury, protection of the interests of workers when employed in countries other than their own, recognition of the principle of equal remuneration for work of equal value, recognition of the principle of freedom of association, the organisation of vocational and technical education and other measures;
>
> Whereas also the failure of any nation to adopt humane conditions of labour is an obstacle in the way of other nations which desire to improve the conditions in their own countries... (Preamble to the Constitution of the International Labour Organization).

Whilst the previous chapter argued for the domestic Justiciability, more general enforceability and the effectiveness of economic and social rights in the form of 'claims' and 'powers', the present one seeks to develop these ideas by arguing for their international Justiciability.[1] At first sight, it might seem that merely to mention labour rights in this connection closes the discussion in favour of their international Justiciability. This is because the global repository of labour rights, the International Labour Organization (ILO), is the oldest institution in the UN family and has long exercised the same semi-judicial role as the human rights committees of the UN. Unfortunately, things are not so simple, and largely because something very similar to the differentiation of justiciable from supposedly non-justiciable rights has happened with respect to international labour rights as in the case of international human rights. And the result may yet be another twist of the double bind that currently afflicts many millions of people in less developed societies. In this case, the differentiation has taken the form of the singling out of seven 'core' conventions as part of the recent, failed attempt by some Western governments, led by the Clinton Administration, to insert a 'Social Clause' into the protocols of the World Trade Organization

(WTO). The seven conventions concern: (1) freedom of association and protection of the right to organise; (2) the right to organisation and collective bargaining; (3) forced labour; (4) abolition of forced labour; (5) discrimination in employment; (6) equal remuneration; and (7) the establishment of a minimum age for employment.

The argument that follows is divided into two parts. The first argues that these core conventions, which are intended to ensure that competition in the rapidly-emerging global economy takes place on a 'level playing field' that allows respect for the fundamental rights of labour, is in fact biased in favour of the 'West' in general, and the United States in particular. The second begins by outlining the current state of play in the debate over what role, if any, labour standards should play in the global trading regime. It then moves on to explain why the current core set should be augmented, and indicates how this might be done in a way that is more sensitive to social differences and would therefore enhance not just the chances of success of any future effort to achieve a Social Clause, but also the more general enforceability of economic and social rights.

The bias that I am concerned with is evidenced by the fact that it would be much easier for Northern governments to ratify and locally enact the core standards than it would be for Southern ones. This automatically, and I am sure unintentionally, presents many Southern societies in a bad light that is not warranted if one takes into account their achievements across the full range of labour standards. That is, most Northern governments have little trouble agreeing that, for example, child labour, gender or racial discrimination in employment, and limitations on freedom of association, are bad things that something can be done about because of the existence of powerful, or at least well-organised, pressure groups within Northern countries. By contrast, in many Southern societies not simply the absence of such groups, but also sometimes the presence of antithetical but nevertheless valued cultural preferences, make it very difficult to agree that such practices are bad, let alone that something should be done about them.

As I will explain in more detail below, what perhaps makes it especially galling for some Pacific-Asian nations, and indeed employers, to see themselves rhetorically disadvantaged in this way is the fact that the current core standards exclude the possibility of any reference to their achievements with respect to other standards outside of the core. These latter are standards that are consistent with their values, supported by their social-structural arrangements, and they generally mitigate the consequences of any derelictions with respect to the existing core. It is therefore unsurprising to me that the majority of Southern nations should have rejected the American-led effort to have the present set of core labour standards included within the protocols of the WTO. However, this rejection was not couched in terms of cultural bias. This also is unsurprising, since, whatever may be the balance of domestic opinion, few nations are prepared to risk being branded in international fora as enemies of freedom, oppressors of children, women and ethnic minorities, or as proponents of slavery and the banning of 'mother's apple pie'. Indeed it is precisely in producing this risk that the discriminatory rhetorical power of the present core shows itself. Instead, the opponents of the Social Clause stressed their fear that it might be invoked for protectionist purposes or in order to justify interference in their domestic affairs. Unfortunately, this tack only made it seem that they had something to hide. In my view, because of the biased nature of the proposal, the fear of international interference was better grounded than the fear of protectionism. The fear of protectionism could be easily assuaged through the setting up of a properly representative, multilateral sanctions committee—such a committee would surely be more alert to the dangers of protectionism than those operating within the context of the present unilateral Generalised Systems of Preferences (GSPs) of the United States and the European Union. However, if the core had been approved, it would have been very difficult both to change it subsequently as well as to resist the intrusions of WTO emissaries intent on enforcing it and unable to accept mitigating arguments based upon achievements with respect to other standards because they were outside their remit.

On the other side of the debate, it seems to me that the International Confederation of Free Trade Unions (ICFTU) were equally ill-advised in their support for the proposed core. In their case, they were seduced by both its apparently common sense, or 'apple pie', character and, very understandably, by the fact that it protected their role. Thus the unions saw the core as supportable because in protecting their role it was 'enabling' in that it allowed for local and future improvements in labour's rights. However, as the preceding chapter suggested, and also for reasons that will be outlined below (see p 76), it is sometimes very difficult for unions to turn formal 'enablement' into actual achievements, and very often unions have to depend upon sympathetic and/or politically dependent governments to secure improvements in labour's rights by improved 'claims' and enhanced 'powers'. In sum, then, it seems to me that the trade union side has reason to be grateful that the draft Social Clause was rejected, since it would have severely limited its strategic options in seeking to improve labour conditions.

The construction of an Ameri-centric core

In order to justify my point concerning the biased nature of the existing set of core labour standards, I will now provide a very short historical account of how they came to be so designated. Although the Preamble (see above, p 69) to the Constitution of the ILO was drafted by a commission presided over by the then President of the American Federation of Labor, Samuel Gompers, it more accurately reflected the consensus between Western European employers, employees and politicians than between their American equivalents. This was because there was no consensus as regards the 'labour question' on the American side, as became very clear when President Wilson lost the election of 1920 and the new Republican Administration refused to seek ILO membership. This also explains why all but one of the 86 ILO conventions adopted prior to

1948, which was when the Convention on Freedom of Association was adopted, related to the protective measures or claims sanctioned by the communitarian values that comprised the Western-European consensus.

Although freedom of association had been included in the Preamble as a means of alleviating 'injustice, hardship and privation', and was strongly desired by the trade unions, it was given no special status vis à vis the protective claims, either through its position in the listing of preferred means or through any textual gloss where it does appear. This changed in 1946, when the ILO adopted a new constitution that incorporated just such a gloss through its inclusion as an annex to the Declaration of Philadelphia, which had been agreed by the 1944 ILO Conference. By this time, the United States had been a member for 10 years and, not surprisingly given its role as the 'arsenal of the free world', its influence is very much in evidence throughout the Declaration. Amongst the most obvious signs of this influence are the identity and ordering of the 'fundamental principles' contained within the Declaration, which privilege the post-New Deal American consensus by deriving labour's case for special consideration from what has always seemed to me to be the curiously romantic—but because of the Sherman Anti-Trust Act of 1890, legally necessary—American statutory declaration (Clayton Act, 1914) that 'labour is not a commodity'. Labour is bought and sold, which makes it manifestly a commodity. Moreover, it has also always seemed to me that Karl Marx was much closer to the mark when he argued that what he termed 'labour power' rather than labour was not only a commodity under capitalist conditions, but one that it was particularly unfortunate to be dependent upon since its exchange value was basically determined by its reproduction costs rather than by the prices its products could command.

Be that as it may, the Declaration of Philadelphia then moves on to state, in the manner of the National Labour Relations Act (NLRA) or Wagner Act of 1935, that 'freedom of expression and of association are essential to sustained progress'. Again, it is perhaps worth repeating why the Wagner Act so emphasised freedom of association, since such a stress is uniquely American. Despite the fact that the United States had been a British colony, and had maintained its commitment to the Common Law after achieving its independence, the British route to the legal empowerment of labour was not available in the United States. This was not so much because there was no electoral majority for it, but more because, as explained in the preceding chapter, in the latter half of the 19th century the Supreme Court managed to read laissez-faire into the Constitution and so was hostile to any forms of collective action that might interfere with freedom of contract. By the 1930s, this hostility had lessened somewhat, but was still strong enough to make the framers of the NLRA aware that they had to ground it in a constitutional principle of greater venerability and cultural resonance than the antagonistic, judge-made one of laissez-faire. Although it was much less obvious that this should be the case in the 1930s than it seems today, they found this alternative principle in the First Amendment to the Constitution which includes freedom of association, and indeed it proved to be of great help to the lawyers who had to defend the constitutionality of the act when it was indeed challenged (Woodiwiss, 1990, Chapter 5).

Other obvious textual signs of American influence in the Declaration of Philadelphia are the stressing of individual equality of opportunity when the Western European states were domestically stressing what might be termed 'collective equality of opportunity', and the requirement, anticipating the 1947 additions to the preamble to the amended NLRA, that the ILO should consider 'all relevant economic and financial factors' before making its decisions and recommendations. Of course, much of the rest of the Declaration makes it clear that the European protective agenda was still in place, and, indeed, had been broadened to include the social-democratic aspiration to achieve 'the extension of social security measures to provide a basic income to all in need and comprehensive medical care'. In sum, what the passing of the Philadelphia Declaration 1944 meant was that, long before the rise of the neo-liberalism associated with Reaganism, the cultural substratum that governed the ILO's 'judgments' was thenceforth no longer simply the communitarianism of Western European societies wherein labour was relatively powerful, but also the only slightly qualified individualism of an American society that tended to regard powerful trade unions as a mark of a social and economic failure to modernise (Woodiwiss, 1990b); hence the United States' government's difficulties in accepting the *bone fides* of Soviet and East European employers' representatives during the 1950s and 1960s. Hence, too, its related withdrawal from the ILO between 1977 and 1980 because of what it saw as the ILO's excessive partiality towards the labour interest. And hence, finally, its understandable and not at all disingenuous singling out of the seven core conventions when it made its Social Clause proposal at the WTO.

The primacy of the ethical dimension

The first thing to say about the debate provoked by the Clinton proposal is that it is in a sense a re-run of an earlier debate that took place in the course of the discussions that led to the formation of the ILO in 1919. The 1919 debate, like the current one, essentially related to the issue of enforcement, and turned on whether or not International Labour Conference resolutions, and especially conventions, should be obligatory on members and therefore have superior legal status to national legislation. Support for the granting of supranational legislative powers to the Conference came from the French and Italian governments' delegations as well as the union delegates. In the event, however, the majority of delegates decided to limit the obligations incumbent upon member states to consideration by their legislatures of whether or not to ratify and locally enact the conventions passed by the Conference. Rather obviously, then, if still rather surprisingly given the recent hegemony of neo-liberal ideas in the United States, the current debate arises out of the Western nations' dissatisfaction with this rather reserved exercise of international legislative power and the consequently similarly reserved mode of enforcement: members who fail to enact conventions have simply to provide their reasons, and members who fail to fulfil their obligations under conventions that they have ratified merely risk having to respond to a negative ILO report (Johnston, 1970, pp 97–106; Swepston, 1992).

The current Western view is that, in the interests of fair competition, both entry into and participation in the WTO system of tariff management and reduction should be conditional upon ratification and enactment of the core ILO standards, and any violations should be punished by trade sanctions. The majority Pacific-Asian and Southern view, on the part of employers and governments, if not unions (Ago, 1995), is that the imposition of such standards would be both inappropriate because of these nations' lower level of development, and unfair because it would deprive them of their major comparative advantage, namely their relatively low labour costs. In sum, on the one hand, Western governments see a strengthened system of international labour standards as a universal benefit, in that it should lead to both an improvement in the conditions of labour in the South and the prevention of the 'race to the bottom' in terms of wages and conditions that their own electorates fear may be the consequence of globalisation. On the other hand, their opponents see any such strengthening of labour standards as something that would serve only selfish, Western political and economic interests.

Drawing on the work of other scholars (Bhagwati and Hudec, 1996; Freeman, 1994; Golub, 1997; Krugman, 1997; OECD, 1996; Rodrik, 1995), Eddy Lee (1997) has recently shown with particular clarity that the jury is still out on the merits of the economic cases made by the two sides. Not being an economist, I am in no position to disagree with this judgment. The result is that, like Lee, I believe that, in the absence of strong economic arguments either way, the more purely moral dimension of the debate becomes the most salient one (see also Sen, 1999b). At this level, Western governments argue that there can be no problem since the standards at issue are universal, not only because they were promulgated by the internationally representative International Labour Conference, but also because they have in all cases been repeated in the various global human rights texts. Two main points are, or could be made by, the opponents of the clause. First, the real rather than formal representativeness of the Conference has always been questionable, given the different levels of financial clout possessed by the various delegations. Secondly, to invoke human rights, especially civil and political rights such as freedom of association, is to compound the problem, since the pre-eminence accorded such rights over social, economic and cultural rights represents an instance of Western cultural imperialism.

The result of this impasse was that the WTO referred back the labour standards issue to the ILO at its 1996 ministerial meeting in Singapore. The ILO's response has been to mount a very energetic and partially successful campaign to have the core ratified by more member states, and to gain the ILO Conference's support for a new 'Declaration on Fundamental Principles' which again stresses the core. Beneficial though these efforts undoubtedly are, the fact remains that international labour standards still lack the teeth that their inclusion in a WTO Social Clause would give them, and which, unfortunately, are still necessary given the activities of those unscrupulous employers and governments who seek a competitive advantage by abusing the human rights of their employees no matter what form these rights take. Moreover, 43 ILO member states from the South and Pacific Asia chose to abstain rather than support the new Declaration. Thus it seems to me that if the abstainers' concerns could be assuaged it would not only be worth trying again for a Social Clause but there would also be a good chance of its successful adoption.

Towards a hybrid core

At this point I would like to draw again on the work (Woodiwiss, 1998) informing the ideas set out in the preceding chapters, since these ideas suggest some ways in which the global appropriateness of any Social Clause might be better assured. This work convinced me that, as in the case of human rights more generally, neither side in the debate has thought hard enough—more specifically, sociologically hard enough—about the issues involved. Moreover, it is my view that, had those involved in the debate thought sociologically harder, they would have discovered that the difference between the two sides is a lot smaller than they currently imagine. My reasons for saying this are twofold. First, ironically, the cultural differences between Western and non-Western societies, whilst considerable in respects that have been neglected, are far less marked as regards the features that have been focused upon in the debate. Secondly, if we assume, as I think we must, that the desire for social justice is equally strong on both sides, then when the full range, rather than the so-called core, of ILO conventions is considered, they provide an excellent basis upon which any remaining differences, and there are some, may be reconciled.

As regards the first point, my principal argument is that the present appearance of great cultural differences is an artefact of the highly generalised, stereotypical models that have been used when, for example, Western and Pacific-Asian values have been compared. That is, typically Western values have been represented as strongly individualistic and liberal, whilst their Pacific-Asian equivalents have been represented as communitarian and statist, if not downright illiberal or authoritarian. Now, the first representation seems to me to be far closer to the value reality of the United States than that of Western Europe, which has long been communitarian, statist *and* rights-based, whilst, on the other hand, individualism and liberalism, and therefore rights discourse, represent a far more influential dimension of non-Western values than some non-Western business and political leaders have been prepared to acknowledge so far.

As was made clear in the previous chapter, the social differences that nevertheless remain have to do with the much stronger resonance that familialist values have in the routines of Pacific-Asian societies on both sides of the labour contract. What this means on the good employers' side is a deep fear of disorder, and even a sense of personal failure to fulfil one's social obligations, that the occurrence of a strike, for example, might produce. What it means on the labour side is an equally profound reticence when it comes to taking action that might be construed as disloyal to a respected superior. The result is that the less scrupulous, culturally opportunistic governments and employers have had some success in branding the proposed core labour standards as an alien cultural intrusion. As significantly, the post-colonial histories that I have looked at in other work (Woodiwiss, 1998) suggest that, even where labour has been granted the core rights, it has not been able to make much use of them. Thus unions have not developed in step with the economy. Of course, there are many other reasons for the failure of unions to develop apart from these inhibiting political and cultural factors. These include the still very large rural surplus populations in many Southern and Pacific-Asian societies, and most pertinently in the current context, the fact that it is very difficult to bring local collective bargaining to a successful conclusion where companies participate in the earlier and simpler links of global commodity chains, whether these are buyer-driven, as in much of the apparel industry, or producer-driven, as in the electronics industry. This point is reinforced once one notes that, for example, a substantial amount of industrial production in the Pacific-Asian countries takes place in Export Processing Zones (EPZs) where, amongst many other advantages, Western and Japanese multinational producers, especially, benefit from the suspension of numerous domestic labour laws.

I would like to turn now to my second and more positive point concerning the advantages of thinking in terms of the full range of labour standards rather than the core, if one wishes to overcome the problems created by the cultural differences indicated by the greater resonance of familialism in Southern and Pacific-Asian societies. Here, my thinking was strongly affected by the discovery reported in Chapter 3 that, although the core freedom to associate, as well as that to organise and bargain, have been greatly restricted in many non-Western societies, there have been compensations through the translation of this 'liberty' into the 'claims' represented by enhanced protective standards and the development of social policy, at least where democracy and the rule of law have been in place. In Japan, these take the form of the Labor Standards Law and a legally-developed right to 'lifetime employment'. In Hong Kong and Singapore, they take the form of very good individual contracts of employment that incorporate many elements derived from the more protective ILO conventions and, especially in the case of Singapore, very substantial citizenship rights with respect to housing and education. Even in the benighted Philippines, strenuous and largely successful efforts were made by a badly under-resourced Department of Labor and the trades unions to enforce a minimum wage between the mid-1950s and the declaration of martial law in 1972.[2]

It is also the case, again to repeat, that it is the form that the non-Western restrictions to freedom of association take—a preference for enterprise unions, for example—that has troubled many in the West rather than their existence as such. This, of course, is because restrictions on the freedoms to associate, organise and bargain have also been imposed in the West, and sometimes for the same ILO-sanctioned reasons (see the Preamble reproduced at the head of this chapter), namely the prevention of economic and social disorder. Examples of such restrictions include: closed shop and/or union no-poaching agreements, the prohibition of communist-led organisations, excessively weak recognition procedures, the absence of employer obligations to bargain, the prohibition of secondary actions, strict limitations on picketing, and requirements both to hold secret ballots and to give notice before strikes. Moreover, in all Western countries, save the United States, such restrictions have been compensated for in very similar if, unsurprisingly, most often more generous ways. Finally, it should be noted that the society that has the best safeguards in place with respect to the problem of enterprise unions abusing their positions is Japan (Woodiwiss, 1992, p 138). This is because, as explained in the previous chapter, the constitutional right to freedom of association is so unambiguously defined as an individual right rather than a trade union right that alternative and minority unions have successfully sustained themselves against many legal challenges. In other words, Japanese labour law suggests how freedom of association should perhaps be reconfigured in a world where individual employment contracts are becoming more important than collective ones and where co-operation between labour and capital has become more and more necessary, whether in the form of enterprise unionism or co-determination structures. In such a world, individual employees need to feel both that they can have access to union support regardless of whether their colleagues are unionised, and to be sure that in a unionised workplace a co-operative union does not become a sweetheart union. In sum, then, in order to be globally pertinent, freedom of association should be reconfigured so as to protect individual employees against potentially oppressive unions as well as against potentially oppressive employers, even though this challenges the union movement's well-established and, I have to say, historically well-grounded, antipathy towards multi-unionism. Within this conception, then, state-guaranteed individual employment contracts represent enabling conditions, since they enhance employee confidence and so make employees more likely to feel able to engage in collective action for redistributive purposes if they consider this necessary.

The advantages, then, of thinking in terms of the full range of standards rather than the core are numerous. First, it provides a set of internationally-legitimate means with which to reconcile cultural differences. Secondly, these means appear to be culturally acceptable to the better Pacific-Asian employers, and thus call the cultural bluff of their less scrupulous colleagues, since these standards involve no direct challenge to their cultural prerogative as the sources of benevolence. Thirdly, although the compensations I have described have only been obtained where, for a variety of reasons, the labour movement has been relatively strong, the fact that they have proved to be acceptable to employers in the most successful economies of the region ought to reduce the strength of any objections to their being enjoyed by more reticent or less circumstantially advantaged employees. Fourthly, the level playing field' argument deployed by Western governments becomes usable *within* the South in general and not simply *between* it and the West. And, finally, multinationals would be both less able to force a 'race to the bottom', and spared the considerable effort and costs involved in sustaining the Corporate Codes of Conduct, best exemplified by that of the Nike Corporation, necessary to assuage the fears and consciences of their metropolitan consumers (Gibbons, 1998).

The need for 'just and favourable conditions at work'

At least three questions still require answers, however: (1) Which of the more than 180 protective ILO conventions presently in force should be selected for inclusion in an augmented but still manageable new Social Clause? (2) What would the translation formula, so to speak, look like that would enable one to determine whether a particular set of translations had passed the compliance threshold? (3) How legitimate or legally safe would the operation of such a formula be in the light of the principles of international human rights law?

Concerning the first question, an obvious principle of selection suggests itself, namely that, like the existing core, the additional conventions should be those that embody human rights (Leary, 1996), specifically the economic and social rights—to work, just and favourable conditions, health, and an adequate standard of living—in order to balance the current emphasis on civil and political rights. All of these rights overlap with the remit of the ILO. However, pace *The Economist* (see above, p 29), Article 7 of the Convention on Social and Economic Rights—just and favourable conditions of work—and, as a self-evident corollary, ILO Convention 81 on Labour Inspection, seem to be particularly strong candidates to play a critical role in the construction of any translation formula for reasons that will be specified below. Article 7 reads as follows:

> The States Parties to the present Covenant recognise the right of everyone to the enjoyment of just and favourable conditions of work, which ensure in particular:
> (a) Remuneration which provides all workers, as a minimum with:
> (i) fair wages and equal remuneration for work of equal value without distinction of any kind, in particular women being guaranteed conditions of work not inferior to those enjoyed by men, with equal pay for equal work;
> (ii) a decent living for themselves and their families in accordance with the provisions of the present Covenant;
> (b) Safe and healthy working conditions;
> (c) Equal opportunity for everyone to be promoted in his employment to an appropriate higher level, subject to no consideration other than those of seniority and competence;

(d) Rest, leisure and reasonable limitation of working hours and periodic holidays with pay, as well as remuneration for public holidays.

As regards the second question, in my view only derelictions with respect to the Forced Labour Conventions could not be translated into any alternative entitlements. The Minimum Age Convention is anyway very flexible (Servais, 1986, pp 195–96), and the most obvious reason why Article 7 might be expected to play a critical role in the construction of any translation formula is the fact that it repeats two of the existing Core Standards—those requiring the elimination of discrimination in employment. This leaves in need of translation only derelictions with respect to the freedoms to associate, organise and bargain. Here, what also recommends Article 7 as the critical principle of selection is that its requirements are much more specific than the others, with the result that measuring compliance, and therefore compensatory effectiveness, of the translation formula would be relatively easy. Almost all the paragraphs simply require contractual or procedural safeguards to be in place which are reasonably precisely specifiable, and hence readily justiciable, and add little to the costs of employers, if not governments. The latter would clearly have to increase their expenditures on Labour Departments, inspectorates, employment tribunals and such like, but not hugely. Another feature that would reduce still further the possible costs involved is that the language used in Article 7 and, indeed, the cognate ILO conventions, features terms such as 'fair wages' and 'decent living', which clearly imply local rather than international points of comparison.

The final reason for regarding Article 7 as critical is politics. Without Article 7's inclusion in a revised Social Clause, any judgment of labour standards in the non-West is likely to be negative. However, with it, not only would some countries in Pacific Asia in particular look better, and many others be made to live up to their own self-chosen standards, but also some Western societies, notably the United States, would look worse. It may surprise some readers to learn that one of the societies that would have most need to make use of any translation formula under paragraph (d) of Article 7 would be the United States, where individual employment contracts are legally largely unregulated in this respect (Summers and Grodin, 1993, p 184). Thus, from the point of view of the South and Pacific Asia, the augmentation of the core would be attractive not simply in acknowledging their cultural particularity, but also by posing a balancing challenge to the United States, albeit a small one.

Finally, turning to the third question, pertaining to the legal legitimacy of the operation of any translation formula, I will simply make two points. First, as made clear in Chapter 2, the translating of the freedoms to associate, organise and bargain into contractual and welfare enhancements has long been accepted as politically and culturally legitimate in Western Europe. Secondly, as explained in the Introduction (see above, p 5), the development and deployment by the European Court of Human Rights of the doctrines known as the 'margin of appreciation' and the 'effectiveness principle' both suggest that such translations could be seen as acceptable when judged against the principles of international human rights law.

Conclusion

In conclusion, then, the Clinton Administration deserves full credit for insisting that any new global trading regime should be premised upon respect for labour's human rights, even though it was unaware of the partial nature of its conception of what these might be. However, and whatever their given and, indeed, non-given reasons, many of the Southern objectors to a Social Clause, and, indeed, to the ILO Declaration on Fundamental Principles, also deserve credit rather than obloquy for at least four reasons. First, global institutions like the WTO and the ILO should not privilege one set of values over another, but should instead be leaders in the formation of a new, plurally defined global ethic. Secondly, continued debate over a possible Social Clause provides an excellent opportunity to demonstrate that such an ethic need be neither non-justiciable nor in any strong sense culturally relativistic, since a more plurally defined set of core standards chosen from the existing array of 180 or so would be both legally binding and enforceable as well as represent a more truly cosmopolitan standard. Thirdly, the effectiveness of the initial draft of the Social Clause in enhancing the human rights of Southern employees would have been minimal, since such enhancement depends not a jot on formal governmental ratification, but instead upon its provisions being embeddable, and therefore enforceable, within local social conditions, which the draft provisions manifestly were not. Finally, several of the objectors to both the draft clause and, indeed, the Declaration could have supported them in far better faith than many who did, but either had no intention of being bound by them or, more often, had little hope of enforcing them because of the weakness of their state institutions. Such objectors in particular deserve credit for risking the wrath of, or—in some ways worse—being patronised by Western governments for whom the rights and wrongs of the issue appeared to be disturbingly clear.

The present Core Labour Standards are the product of a particular history, and their recent rejection as an element in the global trading regime suggests not so much that there is no place for them, but, rather, that it is time to take that history one step further and reconstruct the core on a still justiciable but more equal cultural basis. No other single case produces more compelling reasons for this reconstruction than that of China. This is not simply because of that country's size, position in the world market and rapidly-growing geopolitical status, but also because its present labour rights regime would not pass the test represented by the current core. Thus, absent any such change in the core, as suggested above, China's recent admission to the WTO seems likely to elicit the repetition of accusations of Western self-interest and hypocrisy and, therefore, a further reduction of mutual trust.

Notes

1 An early draft of this chapter was delivered at a conference on 'Labour Relations in Asia and Europe' organised by the Asia-Europe Foundation (ASEF), the International Institute for Social History, the International Institute for Asian Studies, and the Nordic Institute for Asian Studies. It was held at the Dutch Foreign Ministry in The Hague in October 1998. I am very grateful to my fellow conference participants for their many useful comments. The papers from the conference have been published in Koh and van der Linden (2000).
Although the analysis that follows is the product of the same Foucaultian mode of analysis as that carried out in Chapter 1, I have not presented it in the same way in order to avoid a lot of repetition. My knowledge of the history of the ILO is largely derived from the following sources: Cassese, 1990; Charnovitz, 1987; Johnston, 1970; Murphy, 1994; Osieke, 1985.

2 In making this point, I am not, of course, saying that these translations are necessarily adequate, nor that more should not be done to secure freedom of association (see the discussions of Hong Kong, Singapore and the Philippines in Woodiwiss, 1998), but only that the overall balances of imperfections in at least some of these labour rights regimes are not qualitatively worse than those in many Western societies, notably those in Britain (Ewing, 1994) and the United States, where, in particular, the process of union recognition leaves much to be desired (Weiler, 1990).

Chapter 6
Making labour rights justiciable in China

In Chapter 2, I argued that if the enforceability of international human rights discourse was to be enhanced, a way had to be found to recognise the social-structural and cultural particularities of the states parties to which that discourse applies. In Chapters 3 and 4, I identified, for labour rights at least, a process of internationally transparent and democratically approved socio-legal translation made possible by a broadened, but nonetheless justiciable, conception of human rights as one means of achieving this recognition. In Chapter 5, I suggested how such translations might be made internationally enforceable. In this chapter, I will outline how such a translation might be justified in the case of the People's Republic of China.

The requirement for democratic approval specified in Chapter 4 as essential to the legitimacy of a familialist human rights regime would create great difficulties for extending the translation option to the single most important case to which it might apply—China, since there is no way in which that society's current political arrangements may be judged to be democratic. This is, of course, because these arrangements rest neither on free, competitive elections nor on the pertinent rights set out in the International Covenant on Civil and Political Rights (ICCPR). Moreover, in its most considered, and as yet not fully superseded, official statement (White Paper on Human Rights, 1991) the Chinese government is very forthright not only that it values economic and social rights over the civil and political ones that are intrinsic to liberal-democracy, but also that it does not share the Western view of the necessarily pre-eminent role of the legal system in securing rights, and, finally, that it views any attempt to dissuade it or its population from these positions as gross interference in its internal affairs (but see Shih, 1999, Chapter 5 and Kent, 1999, Chapter 5, for accounts of the debate that followed, and the subsequent 1995 White Paper for the changes that resulted). It is therefore both very surprising and sociologically impressive that it is in the area of labour rights that the Chinese government appears to be moving most quickly in the direction of making its rights regime justiciable. It is surprising because the government's record with respect to at least the economic and social rights of the urban labour force represents the best evidence in support of its positive claims as regards its human rights record. Since 1983, and for reasons that will be outlined below, China has been shifting from, in many ways, a generous but ultimately unenforceable labour rights regime based on 'powers' and 'claims', to a legally, if not politically, enforceable variant of the same regime which is, formally at least, very similar to that existing in Hong Kong. It is sociologically impressive because, as will also be explained in more detail below, this remarkable reversal of apparently still sacrosanct principle was brought about by internal forces, combined with the pressures and promises of the transnational—especially economic—forces, that finally forced the Chinese door open in 1979, and the continuous promptings of the International Labour Organization (ILO) (Kent, 1999, Chapter 4).

Writing at the end of the 19th century, Sir Henry Maine famously summarised the history of English law at that time as a journey from 'status to contract'. By this he meant that, whereas under feudalism social relations between individuals were governed by the latter's positions in the various patriarchalist hierarchies that constituted feudal society, under mature capitalism they had come to be governed by the legalisation of the willed relations between autonomous individuals. Maine's aphoristic phrase may also be used to summarise the history of labour law more specifically, except that in the present context it is important to add two elaborations. First, as I have made clear elsewhere (Woodiwiss, 1990a, b; 1992), contract came late to the employment relation as compared to other aspects of economic life, since it took a long time and many changes in other sets of social relations, notably those summarisable as the rise of liberal democracy, before employers could be made to recognise the need for labour to possess collectively exercisable rights if contractual relations between labour and the intrinsically collective employers were to be regarded as equally willed on both sides. Secondly, as was made clear in the preceding chapters, subsequent developments, not just in Britain but also throughout the world, have involved the return of many different forms of status to labour law in the form of 'claims' and 'powers'. However, these 20th century statuses are the inverse of those characteristic of feudalism, in that they are intended solely to protect those in lower positions from suffering the full consequences of the new hierarchy produced by capitalist economic relations.

I mention all of this because I believe it to be useful in helping us to grasp the complexity and significance of what is currently happening in China with respect to labour rights (cf Josephs, 1990, pp 11–13). There, too, Maine's summary is applicable, but the significance of the transformation to which it refers is different in at least one highly significant particular. That is, although the status system—the 'iron rice bowl'—that the introduction of what I will term the Employment Contract Law (ECL) has displaced was paternalistic, like that of many late feudalisms, it was also egalitarian, unlike that of any feudalism (for the difference between paternalism and patriarchalism or familialism, see Woodiwiss, 1998, p 2).[1] It was paternalistic because a party that came to power through a revolution thereafter established itself as the politically unchallengeable master of the Chinese house. However, it was also egalitarian, in that not only did the benevolence of the Party-State involve the granting of many non-wage benefits corresponding to the rights listed in the International Covenant on Economic, Social and Cultural Rights (ICESCR), but also, officially at least, this benevolence was distributed according to meritocratic criteria and its delivery was enforced by the state-controlled trade unions.

The second major difference between the transformation to which Maine refers and that presently occurring in China is that in the latter case, an element of democratic-capitalist law that arrived late in the West—namely the employment contract—has been put into place before the completion of the larger system of capitalist production and law which, moreover, may never be fully installed in China. In the West, it was this longer established and encompassing system that logically required the contractualisation of the employment relation if the law as a whole was to be an internally consistent intellectual structure capable of producing independent judgments on the part of the judiciary (Woodiwiss, 1987b). In China—although since the 1980s the national and local Party-State has dramatically reduced the occasions upon which it exercises possessory and control power within the enterprise (Steinfeld, 1998, Chapter 2; Walder, 1994, 1998)—it has not entirely ceased to exercise such power, and it continues to insist on both its right to hold title in urban land and to exercise general 'supervision' with respect to all property use. What in China are termed 'use rights' with respect to urban land may be leased by non-state entities and private individuals for varying terms according to their use—40 years in relation to commercial uses, 50 years in relation to industrial uses, and 70 years in relation to residential uses. All such leases are renewable but at whatever are the market prices at the time of renewal. Thus, like Singapore and Hong Kong, where the state also holds title to all land and several enterprises, the Party-State continues to possess a significant economic as well as political capacity to shape the substantive content of legal doctrine and policy more generally in the 'public interest', and in ways that do not necessarily privilege the managers of, and shareholders in, enterprises. However, the employment contract has also been introduced without the co-presence of the liberal-democratic institutions of governance that in other societies have allowed employees a say in guaranteeing and controlling the content and effects of this shaping, namely an independent court system and a democratic polity respectively. Moreover, the fact that economic growth has been much faster in some regions of China than others has meant that many millions of people have migrated to areas where, as outsiders and because of the traditionally inspired household registration system *(Hukou)*, despite recent reforms (Zhao, 2001) they can still seldom invoke any of the still-recognised social 'claims' of established residents in respect of housing, health care and education for their children.

In sum, then, and at first glance, it would seem that the ECL is bound to fail as a source of rights for individuals. The new 'claims' that have been established in the form of portable unemployment and health insurance, let alone housing entitlement, are minimal and not yet even fully operational (Josephs, 1990, pp 55–58; Kent, 1993, pp 198–204; Levine, 1997, pp 120–26; Logan, Bian and Bian, 1999; Ng and Warner, 1998, p 68). Moreover, state institutions and the trade unions currently unevenly enforce both these and the newly introduced contractual rights. In addition, the judiciary has as yet no clearly independently generated doctrinal means of judging the fairness of the contractual relation and the rights and duties that the new law may reasonably be seen to give rise to. This is because the employer side, except in the case of solely foreign-owned and private companies, is not wholly legally constituted as capital, and therefore not regarded as inherently economically advantaged in a way that unambiguously justifies protective measures on the labour side. On the contrary, as was still the case at the time of writing, the employer side—in the form of state, military, provincial or local government enterprises, and the joint ventures or partially shareholder-owned enterprises which they participate in—is most often constituted as an element of the national patrimony or collective property, at least at the level of title. Thus it necessarily possesses a superior status to any employee or group of employees and this status will tend to pre-empt the possibility of judicial relief in relation to any claims or complaints employees may have, since such wholly or partly state-owned enterprises are defined in advance as committed to the best interests of the whole people. Finally, the ECL would seem bound to fail as a source of employee rights because, in the absence of liberal-democracy and/or independent trade unions, employees have no autonomous means of influencing how such enterprises deploy their segment of the national patrimony or distribute any surplus that may accrue amongst the competing claims on it. In sum, when considered abstractly, the ECL would seem to portend a condition of industrial absolutism rather than one of industrial justice.

In order to determine whether such pessimism is warranted, most of the remainder of this chapter considers the situation in Guangdong Province, which is where the employment contract system has been most widely and effectively introduced. Thus what follows is divided into five parts. The first outlines the Chinese view of human rights. The second provides an account of the 'iron rice bowl' system which, with variations in its internal dynamics and coverage, was in place by 1956 and against which the character of the new system, with which it currently coexists in most provinces, may be defined. The third describes the economic developments that have placed Guangdong in the forefront of the effort to introduce a justiciable system of labour rights. The fourth outlines the development of the ECL and its legislative twin, Company Law (CL), and describes their content. The fifth presents the results of a study undertaken by the author under the auspices of the Guangdong Provincial Academy of Social Sciences which focused on the workplace and arbitrators' experience of the new system. With regard to the workplace, I was particularly interested in the extent to which the discourses of production—the ways in which both sides of the employment relation think about it (Woodiwiss, 1990a, Chapter 2)—does or does not correspond to the picture of how things should be as projected by the ECL. More specifically, my concern was with the extent to which the ECL is socially embedded and therefore provides an effective means of ensuring industrial justice. With regard to the latter, the focus was on identifying the sources that arbitrators draw upon in order to decide what a fair outcome might be to the disputes it considers. In the conclusion, I provide a necessarily incomplete and preliminary assessment of the current acceptability of the ECL as an instance of translation between one rights regime and another.

Human rights as an iron rice bowl

As Max Weber (1951) recognised many years ago—and as Ann Kent (1993, Chapter 1; see also Weatherly, 1999) reiterates, drawing on the rich scholarly literature produced subsequently, in her far more recent, comprehensive and exceptionally lucid study of human rights in China—Imperial China was by far the longest established and most sophisticated system of familialist rule that the world has yet seen (see also Chen, 1998; Ren, 1997, Chapters 1 and 2). Although this system contained elements—penal sanctions for the grosser violations of proper conduct and a role for custom in regulating disputes, for example—that in other societies eventually became components of what today would be recognised as law, the principles governing their use in China remained overwhelmingly concerned with the maintenance of social order rather than the guaranteeing of security and justice for individuals. Although intellectually impressive efforts to reverse this emphasis were made by various scholars during the period between the fall of the Qing dynasty in 1911 and the Chinese Communist Party's (CCP's) assumption of power in 1949, they were rendered moot by the political and military chaos caused by civil war and the Japanese invasion.

Thus, depending on Kent's detailed analysis, but radicalising her argument in a way that I should acknowledge she may well not find acceptable, it was not at all surprising that the communist constitutions of 1954, 1974, 1979 and 1982 stressed economic and social rights over civil and political ones, since the Party still clearly thought in a traditional Chinese way about the social role of law, and therefore was primarily concerned to specify and re-specify the nature of the social order in the light of changing political priorities and circumstances (see also Ren, 1997, part 2). Moreover, it was not hypocritical for the CCP to include in the same constitutions guarantees of such civil and political freedoms as those of speech, press, association, assembly, and religious belief despite their frequent violation, especially during the Cultural Revolution of 1965–76. This is because, reflecting its Marxism, the CCP regarded such 'bourgeois freedoms' as important only insofar as they were useful in the struggle for the social and economic rights intrinsic to socialism, and as therefore bound to diminish in significance as the struggle progressed. And progress it did, as the 'iron rice bowl' system was established with remarkable rapidity (Kent, 1993, pp 67–78).

The basic parameters of the 'iron rice bowl' system were in place by 1956, at which time the vast majority of the urban, industrial labour force lost the freedom to choose their own employment and were assigned by the central or local state to either large, state-owned and usually heavy industrial enterprises or small, handicraft and consumer oriented co-operatives.[2] The permanent employees in the former sector were the clearest beneficiaries of the new system, in that they enjoyed higher wages, numerous fringe benefits and, except in the case of those found guilty of criminal or political offences, almost inviolable job security. Moreover, they were also allowed to pass on their jobs to their children. The fringe benefits involved included: industrial injury and disability insurance; health insurance for employees and their families; death benefits; maternity benefits; old age pensions; redundancy payments; cost of living supplements; paid home leave; reimbursement of transfer expenses; access to company and government housing; the use of company welfare facilities as well as access to company supplies of consumer goods; and finally the privilege of urban residency and therefore access to the more diffuse benefits of urban life such as better health care facilities, educational opportunities, and a richer cultural life than in countryside. Temporary employees in the state-owned sector as well as co-operative employees enjoyed a somewhat less generous version of the same system.

In addition to access to these benefits being determined by employment status and kind of enterprise, it was also determined by an employee's relationship to the party apparatus in the workplace. That is, party functionaries and those ordinary workers identified by the supervisors of their work groups as activists enjoyed privileged access to all the non-insurance-based benefits—especially those, like promotions and housing, that depended largely on party recommendations. This was justified as a reward for their *biaoxian* or display of commitment to socialist principles as defined by the Party at any particular point in time. In the 1960s, the tension between work performance and *biaoxian* as criteria upon which to base rewards became explicit when stress on the former was identified with 'taking the capitalist road', whilst stress on the latter was identified with the Maoism of the Cultural Revolution. The net result of the Cultural Revolution was not only that economic growth and worker income stagnated, but also, ironically, that patron-client relations of a less ideological and more personal kind—*guanxi* (connections)—were greatly strengthened within many workplaces. Managers and, indeed, party officials were not only fearful of exercising their authority in ways that might invite criticism, but also because they too were suffering economically and therefore were only too willing to seek extra effort from the labour force by offering favours in exchange for gifts.

With the fall of the 'Gang of Four' in 1976 and the return of the former 'capitalist roaders' led by Deng Xiaoping, strenuous efforts began to try to change this situation and restore economic growth. Substantial wage increases were granted to all workers, the bonus system was restored, and *biaoxian* was redefined so that, in the manner of the 'protestant ethic', work effort became a sign of political virtue rather than the other way round. In addition, state-owned enterprises were granted not only greater managerial freedom but also an entitlement to retain a significant percentage of their profits. However, they appear to have initially used the latter entitlement to still further improve the wages they paid and benefits they offered in order to restore and enhance the loyalty of their work forces. Moreover, other reforms introduced at the same time soon made this response anachronistic, in that not only did the consequent rise of new types of enterprise in the consumer goods sector reduce the value of the inducements that the state-owned enterprises of the heavy industrial sector could offer, but it also cast a very unflattering light on the latter's economic performance. It was in this context, then, that the ECL was introduced as part of a strategy to enhance the performance of the state-owned enterprises by reducing their paternalistic expenditures and so changing their internal modes of economic calculation.

Guangdong and the 'open door'

The wider process of economic reform that eventuated in the introduction of the ECL and the Company Law (CL) began in the countryside in late 1978 with the introduction of the 'household contract responsibility system' (HCRS).[3] Under this system, which is now generalised throughout the agricultural sector, segments of communal land are assigned to families who are able to retain or sell anything that they produce once they have met their communal quota, contributed to communal services and paid their taxes. Thanks to a combination of additional administrative and legal measures, the rapidly apparent productivity of the HCRS system, and the consequent reduction in the demand for agricultural labour, a new set of economic entities emerged, again in the countryside, in the form of Town and Village Enterprises (TVEs). These typically light industrial or service enterprises were owned in the name of the people by administrative districts and allowed to produce for the market, pay performance-related wages and retain any profit for investment purposes. In the wake of their success, individually as well as co-operatively owned enterprises also emerged.

Guangdong Province has thus far been by far the greatest economic beneficiary of these changes because of the 'Open Door' policy that was initiated in 1979. In that year, the provincial government established the Special Economic Zone (SEZ) in Shenzhen, which was followed by the establishment of another in Zhuhai the following year, the designation of Guangzhou (Canton) as an 'open city' in 1984, and the creation of the Pearl River Delta Economic Open Area (PRDEOA) in 1985, which included all the above. The PRDEOA was enlarged still further in 1988 and 1993 so that it now has a population of more than 20 million. In this way an extraordinarily dynamic synergy was created between the domestic economic reform process and the desires of foreign investors. Thus, between 1978 and 1993, Guangdong's economy grew at an average annual rate of 13.9%, which was nearly 40% faster than the average for China as a whole. Over the same period, it enjoyed 39.5% of the country's foreign direct investment, and saw its exports grow by an average annual figure of close to 20%. Although investment came from many other sources, notably Taiwan, the lion's share came from Hong Kong as the then colony's companies rapidly shifted their manufacturing operations over the border to take advantage of huge savings with respect to land and labour costs. Similarly, the vast majority of Guangdong's exports went in the first instance to Hong Kong. Between 1978 and 1997, Hong Kong companies established more than 30,000 factories in Guangdong, which currently employ over 4 million people. Initially, most of these operations were engaged in what is referred to as the Outward Processing and Compensation Trade (OPCT), which means that all or most of the material inputs come from overseas and are processed in relatively small, technologically unsophisticated plants before being exported overseas as assembled items. In the 1990s, much larger scale and far more technologically advanced facilities began to be established on the basis of more complex financial arrangements, which included both joint ventures with foreign investors and wholly foreign-owned companies. Of course, the occurrence of such rapid growth in a previously agricultural region meant that the local labour supply was quickly exhausted. The result was that by 1994 there were 6.5 million mainly young, female and single migrant workers in the province, 6 million of whom were employed in the PRDEOA, and many of whom had 'left their posts' in the State-Owned Enterprises (SOEs) of the interior that were struggling because of the new competition. Typically, they presently stay for between three and five years and tend to return home around the age of 25 in order to marry.

Company law, employment law and the justiciability of labour rights

Unsurprising and non-hypocritical though the Chinese stance in relation to rights may be, and remarkable as the improvements in social and economic conditions may have been for many people, any repetition of the suffering inflicted on many thousands of people, including many of today's leading cadres, as a consequence of both the basic stance and the way in which the social and economic gains were made would be clearly unacceptable in the light of the treaty obligations that China anticipates acquiring as a consequence of its signing of the ICESCR in 1997 and of the ICCPR in 1998 (at the time of writing neither treaty had been ratified). Within this context, and despite its clear association with the job insecurity associated with the demise of the 'iron rice bowl' system, the introduction of the ECL and associated legislation into the SOEs in 1983, after having been successfully piloted in the Shenzhen SEZ between 1980 and 1982, equally clearly promised an enhancement of individual employment rights. With the passage of the consolidated Labour Law in 1994, these rights were extended to newly hired employees in 'all enterprises, individual economic organizations...state organizations, institutions, social organizations, and workers in labour contract relations'. Thus, for newly hired employees at least, and including part-time workers, the law for the first time constitutes the employment relation as a contractual one that must be voluntarily entered and may be unilaterally ended, and wherein—and without discrimination of any kind (including against contract workers)—tasks, wages, hours, rest days, training and holiday entitlements, and other conditions, including those relating to health and safety, termination, welfare and social security all have to be specified. Moreover, the law not only requires that the contract should take a written form (for examples see Josephs, 1990, pp 177–92) but also provides for the enforcement of these rights by requiring that employing units set up representative managerial structures and dispute resolution procedures, permitting trade union membership, and establishing state inspectorates (Josephs, 1990; Lauffs, 1995; Lauffs, 1997; Levine, 1997; Ng and Warner, 1998, Chapter 4). By 1996, Douglas Guthrie (1999) reports that 60% of his sample of SOEs in Shanghai had established grievance procedures and 56% mediation committees. Thus, in exchange for losing their security of employment, a majority of Chinese employees will soon and for the first time have individual, legally enforceable rights to certain basic working conditions and welfare rights—on paper at least.

It is plainly still too early to make a final judgment on the extent to which these rights exist on the ground, so to speak. Indeed, Anita Chan's (1998a, b) recent research suggests that there is a still some way to go before they do so exist. Her study of labour conditions in town, village and foreign-owned enterprises in Guangdong and other provinces suggests that migrant workers in particular are subject not only to the myriad discriminations that are a product of the household registration system (Solinger, 1999). Regardless of whether they have a contract but simply because they come from elsewhere, this system denies migrants and/or their children access to local welfare, housing, and educational opportunities. Moreover, they also have to suffer the widespread abuse of their employment rights. Examples of the latter include: the refusal by employers to register their employees with the local Labour Bureau and thereby legalise their position; the demanding by employers of illegal deposits to offset the costs of registration if it is obtained; excessive and unpaid overtime work; wages below the official minimum level; illegal and punitive work rules; and very poor health and safety standards, as well as violence and intimidation.

More positively, both the nature of these abuses—that is, they indicate the still underdeveloped nature of the inspection system—their official acknowledgement (Bao, 1998, pp 70–96; Ong and Baxter, 1999, p 114), and the continuing legislative improvement of formal labour standards which, for example, saw the introduction of the five-day, 40-hour working week and increased holidays in 1997, all suggest that, if it has the will, the government should soon be able to reduce the number of abuses dramatically. Moreover, this impression is reinforced by ongoing developments in company law. China's current company law originated in the need to establish a legal basis for the operation of foreign-funded joint ventures following the opening of its doors in 1979. Initially, therefore, the stress was on securing the ownership rights and limiting the liabilities of overseas investors. Over time, the legislation has been broadened to allow for greater enterprise autonomy by granting managements improved possessory and control rights, as well as sanctioning the encroachment on the state's monopoly of title consequent upon the formation of joint-stock companies which can raise funds on stock exchanges and so incur policy-related and financial obligations to non-state shareholders. Soon all enterprises owned by governmental organs below the county level will be privatised (Ong and Baxter, 1999, p 97), and the official expectation is that in the medium term all but high tech and/or militarily sensitive enterprises will also be privatised (*Sunday Morning Post*, 12 June 1999, p 6). The result is that not only are Chinese companies, like their equivalents elsewhere, required to obey the law, including the Labour Law, but also, as in many European countries, they are required to consult with their labour forces on such issues as salaries, health and safety, work rules, and major production and social insurance issues. Finally, and most distinctively, Article 4 of the CL requires them to 'observe professional ethics, enhance the building of socialist spiritual civilisation, and accept supervision by the government and the general public'(quoted in Ong and Baxter, 1999, pp 96–97). The existence of the latter requirement, and its structural similarity to the 'public interest' clause to be found in many instances of Western legislation, clearly creates the basis for a court to fill in gaps and resolve ambiguities in the law, whilst its specific content suggests that these are likely to be to the benefit of the employees.

Moreover, the ongoing development of company law may also be seen as encouraging not only because it explicitly reinforces the Labour Law, but also because its projected development and further realisation will remove or at least radically diminish two of the principal structural obstacles to proper enforcement. The first is the conflict of interest that occurs when governmental organs are the owners, or in other ways financial beneficiaries, of the enterprises that they are required to police. The second is an obstacle to the juristic clarity necessary if the law is be able to differentiate rights clearly enough to enforce them: this obstacle is the state's ownership of the national patrimony. A further encouraging development on the latter score is the enhanced constitutional status accorded to private property by the various amendments promulgated since 1982. Thus, although the existence of the 'private economy' was only constitutionally recognised in 1982, by 1988 it was accorded the position of a 'complement to the economy of socialist public enterprise', and in 1999 it became an 'important component of the country's socialist market economy'.

All this said, and recognising that, for financial and other reasons, there are limits to how comprehensive and effective any inspection system can be, and as elsewhere, the best candidate for the role as the most mobile and therefore ultimate enforcer of labour rights is the trade union movement. The difficulty, of course, is that in China there is little experience of trade unions as the autonomous enforcers of such rights, whether on the part of the state, employers or indeed the unions themselves. Thus, although according to the Trade Union Law of 1992 and the Constitution of the All-China Federation of Trade Unions (ACFTU) of 1993, unions are enjoined to 'conduct their work in an independent and autonomous way', their role is also defined in the same places as that of the 'bridges and bonds linking the Party and the masses of workers and staff members...[an] important social pillar of the State power'. Their ambiguous position is perhaps best brought out by a brief account of the ups and downs of their right to call strikes. Whilst, the use of the strike weapon has never been encouraged by the government, it was nevertheless included in the 1954 and 1979 Constitutions but excluded from those of 1974 and 1982. Moreover, whilst the ACFTU has never described strikes as illegal *per se*, it does not call them and appears to go along with the rigorous anti-strike policies of such provinces as Guangdong (Lavender, 1997, pp 84–85). Nevertheless, under what has usefully been described as the resulting system of 'state corporatism' (Chan, 1994), the unions have not always exercised their 'powers' by simply performing the passive, 'transmission belt' role assigned to them, which in turn is because workers more generally have not been passive (Sheehan, 1998). Thus they were dissolved in 1967 because their leadership failed wholeheartedly to support the Cultural Revolution, and since their restoration in 1978 they appear to have conscientiously sought to delineate a quasi-autonomous space for themselves within 'bureaucratic politics' from which they could protect the interests of their members amid the stresses and strains of the ongoing process of economic restructuring (Ng and Warner, 1998). Their most general current problem is, however, as Anita Chan (1994, pp 174–77) has pointed out in a most insightful commentary on the contending discourses of the reform era, that the public language that the unions have had to use to enunciate their position sounds too like that of Party 'conservatives'. The consequence is that the unions have yet fully to win the trust of their current membership in the shrinking, state-owned sector of industry, let alone that of their potential constituents in the still largely unorganised foreign-owned and/or private sector.

Nonetheless, despite the absence of the autonomous enforcement power possessed by fully independent trade unions, there are today encouraging signs that labour rights have indeed become justiciable, in that there has been an exponential rise in the number of cases brought before the Labour Arbitration Committees established under the ECL—from 12,363 in 1993 to more than 47,000 in 1996 (Ng and Warner, 1998, p 72; China Statistical Yearbook, 1997; for some early case reports, see Josephs, 1990, pp 193–208). Moreover, despite a strong cultural aversion, shared with Japan, to involving the courts as opposed to mediators and arbitrators (Be, 1996) in solving disputes, not only did some cases rapidly reach the courts, but the results have tended to be positive for the labour side (Josephs, 1995, pp 574–75).

Finally, the fact that the new law, at least initially, did not affect the employment status of established employees who continue to enjoy the privileges of the 'iron rice bowl' system, save for the right to pass on their jobs to their children, means that—at least in the larger SOEs and despite any future privatisations—the basic organisational culture necessary for the nurturing of these rights, in the form of the acceptance of the idea of employees as what in Western Europe would be called stakeholders or social partners in their enterprises, remains in place. However, its meaning and institutional realisation have obviously been made far more uncertain and complex by the fact that this organisational culture has to be made to accommodate two very different systems of employment regulation.

Justiciability in Guangdong Province

In line with Guangdong's pioneering role in other aspects of the reform process, 1996 saw it become the first province to displace the 'iron rice bowl' system altogether and make the contract system universally applicable.[4] Thus by 1998 it was established in 100% of SOEs, 98% of collective enterprises, 70% of foreign-owned enterprises, 60% of TVEs, 40% of private companies, and 30% of individually owned enterprises—the goal for 1999 was that the contract system should be established in 80% of all kinds of enterprise. Employees sign with the legal representatives of companies, whilst the latter sign with the local government. The length of the contract term is negotiable, with one year being the normal but not mandatory minimum and three years the most common term across the province as a whole, whilst employees with 10 or more years' service may sometimes be allowed indefinite terms or to stay on until retirement. Either side may end the contract before it expires, but with compensation to the other party. Employers have to compensate employees for loss of earnings unless termination occurs during the probationary first six months or for reasons of non-work-related illness. Employees may have to compensate employers for the registration fees paid on their behalf, training and replacement costs, and any direct losses consequent on their departure. In the case of workers with skills for which there is a high demand, their new employers will often pay such compensation. Although these requirements might seem unduly stringent and restrictive to Western eyes, the authorities point out that the mobility rate in the province as a whole is nevertheless 25% per year. Also, with many new companies setting up each year, they think that the longer established companies deserve some protection against labour poachers.

Enforcement is achieved through two principal mechanisms derived in part from German, Hong Kong and Japanese models: a pro-active, preventative and inquisitorial inspection system, which is far more developed than in the rest of the country, and a reactive network of arbitration committees to solve disputes. An annual, general province-wide inspection is carried out in the name of the highest political authority, the Provincial People's Congress (PPC), by a body which brings together the Labour Bureau, the social insurance agency and the trade unions, and through the local offices of the Labour Bureau. Companies are required to report on all legally pertinent aspects of their personnel relations. In addition, the provincial government requires its local offices to carry out special inspections at two other critical points of the industrial year: one is shortly before the end of the year—in order to check that wage obligations have been met, and the other a month into the new year—to check that all contracts have been either issued or renewed. The PPC's representatives study these reports, and they are legally empowered both to make site inspections if they have any questions or suspicions and to require compliance. These annual inspections are supplemented by routine local inspections, the requirement that all companies submit a monthly report on the wage payments they have made over the previous three months, and visits in response to employee complaints. The latter may be made in person, in writing or by using telephone hotlines. The responsibility for carrying out most of the work involved in these inspections falls on the shoulders of a labour inspectorate, which is co-ordinated by seven senior provincial inspectors to whom a much larger number of local inspectors are responsible. There are, for example, 20 in Guangzhou (Canton), 30 in the Zhuhai SEZ, and between 50 and 60 in the Shenzhen EPZ. The overall ratio of inspectors to employees is 1:30,000 which the Labour Bureau freely acknowledges is very low when compared to the ratio in Hong Kong, which stands at a much more comfortable 1:5,000.

Like the Labour Bureau of which it is a part, the Labour Arbitration Committee operates at three levels—provincial, city (county in rural areas), and township—but most of its work is carried out at the township level.[5] It not only deals with appeals against the inspectorate's findings, but also with collective and individual disputes. Individual disputes make up 95% of its caseload. The rapid localisation of its activities was considered necessary if the large number of cases it has to consider—some 15,000 per year (30% of the national total)—are to be dealt with quickly and efficiently. Only 10% of cases go all the way to formal arbitration, since 90% are settled at the prior mediation stage. In Dongguan City, for example, which is a major centre of operations for foreign-owned enterprises and where the working population numbers more than 800,000 locals and 1,450,000 migrants, there were 170 inspectors and 160 arbitrators at the time of writing, mainly distributed in groups of two or three throughout the city's various townships. Despite the low ratio of inspectors to employees, 92% of all employees, including 84% of migrant workers, had signed individual contracts with their employers in some 13,000 companies by 1998. Also, in the first six months of 1999, the arbitrators completed 300 mediations and 80 arbitrations, with each arbitrator dealing with one case per day as a yearly average. Those dissatisfied with an arbitration decision are free to appeal against it to a local court if they do so within 15 days. Province-wide, the principal sources of disputes are early or unfair dismissals, employer failures to pay social security contributions, compensation for industrial injuries, and disciplinary matters.

Another very significant enforcement mechanism is that represented by the trade union organisation which, according to one local leader, sees the 'enforcement of the Labour Law as its key work'.[6] Thus, for example, whereas in 1978 when Dongguan City was still a predominantly agricultural area there were only 211 organisational units, by 1999 there were 2,286 (1,140 in foreign-funded enterprises) organising 150,000 members or some 15% of the labour force. Unions apparently readily respond to requests for help from members and other employees, and negotiate on their behalf with employers both directly (sometimes in the context of the 1,250 dispute conciliation committees that exist in the city's enterprises) and as part of Arbitration Commission mediation hearings. In 1998, unions claimed a role in settling some 500 disputes. However, they also engage in preventative measures in the form of educational activities and the negotiating of collective contracts. The latter supplement individual contracts by establishing common conditions for all employees in a particular enterprise, ensuring that at least the minimum wage (350 renmimbi per month in 1999) is paid, hours are regulated, overtime payments made, holidays honoured, as well as that social security, health and safety, and maternity leave obligations are met. By 1999, 470 such contracts had been signed: 283 in SOEs, 178 in foreign-funded, and 9 in private enterprises. A recent union follow-up study of 21 such agreements found that most had been honoured and there had been a sharp reduction in the number of disputes in, or emanating from, the enterprises involved, which in turn had had very beneficiai consequences for the status of the trade union organisation in the city. In addition, Dongguan's unions have successfully negotiated the establishment of the participative structures represented by the Workers' Congresses in 460 mainly state-owned enterprises in order to facilitate, amongst other things, bargaining over improvements in pay and conditions. They also participated in the 'democratic evaluation of managers' in 420—again mainly state or collectively owned—enterprises, and gained 8 places on boards of directors and 13 places on the supervisory boards that exist in some 'experimental modern enterprises'. Finally, the city's unions administer an income support programme for the employees of 'inefficient' enterprises.

Workplace culture and justiciability

In sum, then, a well-organised, multi-layered if not very dense enforcement mechanism has been established in Guangdong, staffed by well-trained officials. All arbitrators, for example, have undergone four years of specialised professional training. However, as stressed in earlier chapters, sheer organisation and even integrity cannot themselves guarantee the effectiveness of an enforcement mechanism, since in the end this depends upon the mechanism's embeddedness, and therefore appropriateness, within the set of social relations it is intended to regulate. In order to make at least a preliminary assessment of the appropriateness of the Guangdong mechanism to its intended object of regulation, and because I knew of no extant studies in English (but see Lee, 1998), I decided to undertake an exploratory, small-scale study of workplace culture in the province.[7] At its core, the interview schedule I constructed for this purpose (see Appendix) asked the interviewees (15 managers and supervisors, 18 ordinary employees, and two corporate professionals) to imagine themselves confronted with three different types of problems—technical, social and personal—and asked them how they would deal with each of them and whether they would solve them on their own or seek help from others, specifically colleagues, supervisors, trade union officials, or managers. The thought behind interviewing managers and supervisors as well as ordinary employees was not only to see if rank made a difference to the answers given but also, since the different ranks came from the same workplaces, to get a sense of the extent to which understandings of the nature of the workplace culture were shared within the enterprise.

The very simple idea behind this strategy was distilled from reading a large number of management and industrial relations studies from around the world, especially an ethnography by the late Filipino sociologist Elias Ramos (1990, Chapter 4). And the idea is that, whereas one would expect employees throughout the world to answer 'supervisor' after 'self in relation to technical problems, one would also expect their answers to diverge with respect to social and personal problems. Specifically, whereas one would expect employees in more familialist cultures like Japan to tend to seek help from supervisors or seniors with respect to social and personal problems (Bennett and Ishino, 1972; Woodiwiss, 1992, pp 87–90), one would expect employees in more individualistic cultures like Britain and other Western European countries (Hickson, 1993) to be far less likely to seek such help from supervisors, preferring instead either to find solutions themselves or to ask colleagues or trade union officials to help.

The significance of this divergence as regards the appropriateness of different modes of enforcement is as follows. A labour rights regime stressing 'liberties', such as freedom of association and the right to strike, may well prove to be very effective in the more individualistic cultures where workplace relations, especially between sub- and super-ordinates, tend to be somewhat distanced and rather strictly instrumental. This is because there is therefore little in the way of vertical ties of social or emotional dependence to provide a basis for resistance to either horizontally organised solidaristic actions on behalf of colleagues, or the involvement of such 'outsiders' as trade unions and labour departments. Indeed, the latter difference may even be internalised—as where unions become 'social partners'. However, such a regime is highly unlikely to be effective in more familialist cultures where vertical ties of social and emotional dependence exist, since not only do they represent a source of resistance to collegial solidarity and union involvement, but they also often pre-empt any such resorts on the part of subordinates. What might make this especially possible in the case of Guangdong is the fact that it is apparently likely that super- and sub-ordinates come from the same town or village, and that the former recruited the latter (Lee, 1998, pp 84–88). The preventive effect of such ties is, of course, why their fostering is usually part of corporate anti-union strategies in the West (Jacoby, 1997). In familialist societies, therefore, since it is unlikely to be present spontaneously, so to speak, ways have to be found to insert rights discourse into the wider discourses of production and ensure that it carries some force within them. All of this suggests that the best way to protect labour from abuse would not be to translate companies' self-acknowledged social and emotional responsibilities into expansively defined individual rights of association and collective bargaining, since these are unlikely to be taken up. Rather, it suggests that the way forward would be to translate these social and emotional responsibilities into 'claims' on the state, provided companies agree not only to be inspected, but also to be contractually—and therefore legally—bound with respect to certain basic, individually pertinent labour standards.

So what, then, is the nature of the workplace culture that the Guangdong labour rights regime seeks to regulate? The first thing to say is that it is, of course, rather varied, since many types of enterprise operate within the province and, indeed, within the city that I studied more closely. Unfortunately, although my sample does adequately reflect the range of industries in the province (toys, food processing, textile printing and five kinds of electrical equipment manufacturers), it does not proportionately reflect the variety of ownership types since, whilst my sample of nine companies includes five foreign-funded enterprises, it only includes two privately-owned ones, one TVE, and one SOE. Thus I will perforce be talking in aggregate terms in what follows. This said, with one perhaps surprising exception that I will point out below, no dramatic cultural differences of the kind I was interested in were apparent amongst the different types of enterprise in the sample on the basis of the interviews. All of the interviewees except two ordinary employees said that they would first try to solve any technical problem themselves and then ask a supervisor if they were unsuccessful. All of the managers and professionals said that it was their responsibility to solve any social problems affecting their employees' performance in the workplace, whilst nine of the ordinary employees said that it was their supervisor's responsibility. Eight of the managers and 10 of the ordinary employees said they would seek a superior's help in solving personal problems. Surprisingly, only one of the largely migrant ordinary employees said that the reason they would turn to someone was because they were a 'hometowner', but this may be because this possibility was not put to them directly. Finally, only five managers and one ordinary employee said they would seek trade union help in solving social and personal problems. However, only six of the managers and two of the ordinary employees worked in companies where a union was present. All in all, and in line with both Lee's (1998) ethnographic and Warner's (1995, Chapter 9) broader studies, this pattern of responses suggests that both individualism and familialism are present in the discourses of production and that, whilst the former is more consistently articulated by managers than ordinary employees, neither is exclusively articulated by one particular side of the industrial divide. Regardless of what transnational cultural influences may be in play, such presences are, of course, not surprising, since socialism as a discourse is an articulation of individualism and familialism mediated and transformed by their joint articulation with egalitarianism.

The presence of familialism was further confirmed, and its somewhat greater influence suggested, by the fact that whereas 11 managers and 12 ordinary employees said that companies should help employees with problems that were outside of their contractual responsibilities, only four managers and six ordinary employees said that they should not. The fact that two of the managers and two of the ordinary employees who answered negatively were employed by the one, and as it happens very profitable, SOE in the sample suggests that the state has approached the task of preparing the SOEs for the rigours of the market very seriously. The majority justified their view by either invoking the metaphor of the family (five times) or ideas of 'humanity', 'morality', 'membership', 'loyalty', 'duty', 'obligation', 'responsibility', or 'social tradition'. Two interviewees, invoked what might be regarded as the more modernistic ideas of 'efficiency' and 'productivity'. Moreover, just over half of all interviewees remembered having raised one or more serious problems with managers or supervisors, whilst five had raised them with trade union officials and four with mediators or arbitrators. All but four of those raising problems pronounced themselves happy with the result. Despite the fact that the vast majority of ordinary employees' contracts were for renewable one- or two-year terms, all of the interviewees declared their employment contracts to be a source of security to them because of the clarity with which their rights and obligations were set out. Moreover, only five managers (four had no contracts) and seven ordinary employees had ever had reason to look at them after they had signed them, and this was as often to clarify things for themselves as to help them resolve problems.

The presence of individualism was confirmed by the finding that only seven interviewees would avoid challenging a superior whom they thought was being unfair to them, whilst 25 said they would challenge the offending superior directly and three would 'quit' immediately! Finally, all but two of the managers confirmed that they had been criticised, in their view unfairly, by their subordinates. None admitted to having any great trouble with this although many said it made them angry.

Finally, the same co-presence of individualism and familialism was apparent in the responses of the even smaller sample of four arbitrators who were asked a separate set of questions (see Appendix). The most common problems brought to them were late pay, failures to pay overtime and redundancy pay, unfair dismissals, injuries, excessive hours, and excessively punitive company rules. Although each of these problems involves a clear contractual breach, the surrounding circumstances sometimes, as in any other jurisdiction, makes the apportionment of fault rather difficult. In such circumstances, the arbitrators freely acknowledged that they invoked common sense ideas in their efforts to achieve mediated settlements. In the words of one arbitrator, these ideas encompassed notions of 'rational behaviour', on the one hand, and 'human considerations relating to feelings and friendships', on the other. At a more general level, they also generally involved, and again on the one hand, reminding the parties of what I will term the 'coldness' of the legal reasoning which would determine the outcome were either one of them to insist on proceeding to a formal arbitration hearing, and, on the other, invoking what appeared to be clearly familialist conceptions of the 'good company'.

Conclusion

At the beginning of this chapter I indicated that, whilst one must be impressed by the scale of what is currently happening in China with respect to labour and, by extension, human rights more generally, one is also entitled to be sceptical as to the likely significance of the out-turn from the point of view of ordinary employees—they have been asked to give up what was in many respects for them, if not the economy as a whole, a 'great deal', in both senses, in exchange for promises of uncertain deliverability. The reasons for this scepticism may be termed the 'three absences', namely those of independent trade unions, the rule of law, and liberal democracy, each of which is critical with respect to the ultimate enforceability of a 'new deal'.

In my view, however, what the preceding analysis allows one to conclude, but only provisionally given its very small scope, is that this scepticism should be qualified.[8] Indeed, given the balance between individualism and familialism in the discourses of production, the triple track approach of a pro-active inspection system to counter the possibly negative effects on enforcement of familialism, the reactive mediation/arbitration mechanism to mobilise and amplify the effects of individualism, and the educative and solidaristic approaches of the Labour Bureau and the trade unions respectively, seems to have been appropriately designed to deal effectively with a highly complex transformation in the nature of the industrial relations system. Thus it appears to have been effective in making labour rights justiciable in a province where this was not so 20 years ago and despite the unpropitious transnational circumstances (see above, p 23). What is far less clear, however, is the status and, indeed, meaning of egalitarianism within the present discourse of rule, as is also therefore the meaning of the phrase 'socialism with Chinese characteristics' (for a subtle account of the role of this phrase within the discourse of rule, see Kluver, 1996). On the one hand, individualism and familialism have regained some of their pre-revolutionary meanings and legitimacy as egalitarianism has been de-emphasised. Indeed, whereas the nationwide measure of inequality known as the Gini coefficient stood at a very low 0.2 in 1978, it had already reached close to Hong Kong's high level in 1994 when it stood at 0.434 (Ng and Warner, 1998, p 166). On the other, however, the Party-State still possesses sufficient political and economic power to ensure, if it so wishes, that all Chinese enjoy equal social and economic citizenship rights. Indeed, as one Labour Bureau official explained to me, the introduction of the ECL was precisely an instance of the use of such power since, in the absence of such a law—and because contractualism is not spontaneously present in Chinese society—employees would have been bereft of any authoritative discursive means to qualify either a resurgent familialism, or a now more thoroughly westernised individualism, within what are increasingly often capitalist enterprises. It would be difficult to think of a clearer illustration of Marshall's point (see above, p 8) concerning citizenship rights as 'instruments of stratification'.

This is not, of course, to say that one can be entirely sanguine about the prospects for labour and human rights in China. This is because not only is the system described above far less developed in most other provinces, but also the scale, complexity and radicalness of the transformation taking place makes it a process fraught with the dangers consequent upon unexpected events. Amongst many possibilities, two that suggest themselves are policy reversals at the behest of politically powerful vested interests who have lost out as a result of the reform process, and risings of one kind or another on the part of the migrant workers who have made the economic breakthrough possible but still find themselves rigorously discriminated against through the residency system. The latter possibility, however, seems to have been realised by the authorities, who now seem to be taking the migrants' need for health care and entertainment, for example, much more seriously than in the past—currently, Guangdong budgets 200,000,000 renmimbi per year for migrant health care and several townships are rapidly constructing new public entertainment spaces. Moreover, migrants marrying locals may now qualify for residency after five years.

In the most general of terms, then, it is the comprehensiveness and systemacity of the government's approach, plus the fact that the regime is very well aware that its legitimacy is at stake, which gives one confidence that it is the reconstruction rather than the dissolution of labour rights that is being attempted (for evidence of widespread labour unrest in the 1990s, see Leung, 1998). Thus what might be termed the 'total institution' (Warner, 1995, pp 45–46) represented by the *danwei* (work unit) that represented the core of the 'iron rice bowl' system has been systematically de-constructed as its autonomy from the Party-State has been increased. Its welfare functions are in the process of being devolved onto the national, provincial and local governments, which are simultaneously ceasing to exercise their former possessory, control and even proprietary rights, whilst legal and quasi-legal institutions take their place. Moreover, trade unions have retained their position in the workplace, or at least their right to one, and because of the withdrawal of the Party-State they are now more likely to behave in the 'independent and autonomous way' sanctioned by the Trade Union Law. This, in turn, should mean that enterprise-level representational and grievance procedures, Labour Arbitration Committees and the courts should all become far more used to hearing variant readings of the meanings of the various rights and duties specified in the Labour Law. The net result should therefore be that, for the sake of their own dignity, legitimacy and institutional growth if for no other reasons, the adjudicatory bodies involved will in time become subject to the discipline of consistency that is central to the rule of law whose future establishment the CCP committed itself to in 1996 (Chen, 1998, Chapter 11; Li, 1997; Keith, 1994; and, more sceptically, Kent, 1999, Chapter 7). Indeed, my sample of arbitrators, who had all been formally trained, made it clear that they were already accustomed to such discipline in that they routinely resorted to legal texts of one kind or another, including court decisions, in order to ensure that their practice was consistent with that of higher *legal* authorities.

In sum, then, it seems to me that there is every reason to think that two at least of the empty social places represented by the 'three absences' will eventually be filled—specifically those pertaining to independent trade unions and the rule of law—as enterprises are capitalised and the Chinese labour rights regime is transformed from one describable as egalitarian paternalism to one which approaches the model of enforceable benevolence. To repeat my most basic point, what, for the sake of effectiveness, this imagined model allows is just such a translation of freedom of association into 'powers' and 'claims' as appears to be constitutive of the emerging Chinese regime. What, however, disqualifies it as an achieved instance of such a regime is the absence of those guarantees of the enforceability of the translation from labour's point of view that are represented by employee choice of union, as is also the case in Singapore, and citizen choice of governing party, as is also the case in Hong Kong. Achieved instance or not, what is nevertheless geopolitically challenging about the Chinese case is the fact that, given the current list of core labour rights, the labour rights regime that appears to be crystallising there is not one that could be internationally recognised as legitimate. Thus, without a change to the core along the lines suggested in Chapter 5, the opening of the new millennium is likely to begin inauspiciously with China's Herculean effort at social re-engineering unappreciated and, given China's entry to the WTO with United States support, the latter power both accused of double-standards with respect to labour rights and unable even to think about using the sanctions inherent in a Social Clause as a potential if limited means of compensating for China's, and indeed many other nations', democratic deficits. Finally, whatever the Party-State's undoubted culpability with respect to other kinds of human rights violations (Kent, 1999, Chapter 7), it is important not to lose sight of the fact that, with the exception of those activists engaged in independent union activity, by far the greatest threat to labour's rights now comes from capitalist enterprises rather than the Party-State.

Notes

1 What I term the Employment Contract Law was first introduced in 1986 as 'Temporary provisions for the implementation of labor contracts in state-owned enterprises'. In 1994 it was formally incorporated into the Labour Law.

2 The following description of the 'iron rice bowl' system is almost entirely derived from Walder (1986), but see also Li and Wang (1996) and Kaple (1994).

3 David Zhao Xiansheng, who has recently completed his doctoral studies in the Department of Sociology, University of Essex, carried out the research for this section primarily on the basis of Chinese language sources.

4 The information contained in this and the following paragraph was provided in an interview with officials from the Guangdong Provincial Labour Bureau.

5 The information contained in this paragraph was provided in an interview with officials from the Dongguan City Labour Bureau, Guangdong.

6 The information contained in this paragraph was provided in an interview with officials from the Dongguan City Trade Union Organisation, Guangdong.

7 I am very grateful to Professors Li Benjun, Liang Guiquan and Zhan Tianxiang, all of the Guangdong Provincial Academy of Social Sciences, for their support and encouragement with this project, which was undertaken in the summer of 1999. Excellent interpreting was provided by Zhao Xiansheng, with equally excellent help and logistical support by Chen Rongping. I am also most grateful to numerous, very well informed officials of the Guangdong and Dongguan Labour Bureaux for their support and very valuable information. In addition, I am not only equally grateful for similar help from the Dongguan Federation of Trade Unions and from the Mayors and leaders of Qingxi and Chang'an townships, but also for superb accommodation, excellent interview facilities and very generous hospitality from the latter. Finally, and of course, I am perhaps most grateful to the anonymous companies and their staff who allowed and found the time for the interviews.

I set the parameters for the sample of companies whilst the actual companies were chosen by the town governments involved. The basis upon which they did this was certainly not random in a statistical sense, but seemed to depend mainly on the availability of personnel. Since the number of companies and individuals that were interviewed was so small, I have presented my results using raw numbers in order to avoid giving a false appearance of the statistical representativeness of my sample.

8 Clearly, before work such as has been reported here could be used to justify any exercise in socio-legal translation, it would have to be repeated on a far larger scale and in a far more rigorous fashion. In particular, closer attention would have to be paid to employees' experiences of the system. Moreover, a series of open-ended and in-depth interviews would be needed to confirm the presence of the individualist and familialist discourses that is suggested by my little survey.

Conclusion
Making work for human rights

The most general argument of this book has been that, if our present array of human rights is seen not as a perfected summation of human aspirations, but instead as a developing disciplinary technology which may be used to protect people from abuse, a way may yet be found of breaking out of the 'human rights box' that currently makes them more useful to the rich and powerful than to the poor and powerless. Of course, the general idea of human rights has a particular genealogy, but the result of acknowledging this should be the eschewal of claims to ideological or civilisational privilege rather than their amplification. Thus, whilst it is clear that the specific concept of rights may be traced back from the grand, 18th century European and American declarations, through William Blackstone's *Commentaries on the Laws of England* and the English common law that it systematised, to the Magna Carta of 1215, and even the Ancient Greek and Roman Republics, this knowledge should be used critically and for reconstructive purposes. It should not be used as a justification for self-congratulation and an excuse for locking the box, as is the case with the current form of the doctrine of 'justiciability'.

This is for at least three reasons. First, as Karl Marx made so clear in his 1843 text *On the Jewish Question*, and as the subsequent necessity of many further rights struggles on the part of multiple social movements has confirmed, the rights most often associated with what might be called the classical genealogy may also be seen as a way of ideologically and legally entrenching an egotistical, white, male, and heterosexist individualism that excludes the possibility of addressing the problems posed by inequalities of various kinds. Secondly, when knowledge of this genealogy is used to interrogate contemporary international human rights discourse, it becomes clear that the Western tradition of rights thinking has, indeed, been disproportionally influential, given that the purpose of the international discourse is the protection of all the world's peoples relative to the actual dangers they face, rather than simply those faced by the population of the West. Thirdly, those who deploy for celebratory purposes knowledge of either the classical, or, indeed, the more broadly-defined post-classical, genealogy display a breathtaking degree of sociological naiveté. That is, they do not see that precisely because of the specificity of such genealogies, the effectiveness of the protections afforded by the rights involved is critically dependent on their imbrication with certain social-structural and institutional forms. Thus, to repeat what was said in the Introduction, there is a tendency for them to think of these rights, once they have been proclaimed, as either self-enforcing or as automatically enforced by whatever institutions exist. In the labour sphere, for example, unscrupulous governments may currently meet US or EU aid conditions by passing a law granting rights to form unions and bargain collectively, which they know full well will be seldom if ever acted upon. However, were the existing US and EU conditions to be applied in the Chinese case, it would be impossible to meet them by showing that individual contracts of employment exist, specify certain basic entitlements, and are fairly and rigorously enforced by a governmental inspectorate that potentially could be internationally held to account. This is because even the new Chinese labour law does not rest on explicitly defined and readily activated freedoms to associate and bargain collectively. Moreover, and more generally, where resources are made available in the form of support for the establishment of Western-style, legal and human rights institutions, the results may not be those that were intended. That is, as seems to be the case in Africa, because of their relatively high salaries and access to modern transport and communications technologies, even local activists may come to be seen as part of an alien, international political class rather than as defenders of the less powerful in the localities where they operate (Odinkalu, 2000).

The reconstructive lesson I derive from this critique is that, only once international human rights discourse has been freed from ethical imperialism will it be fully capable of providing the basis for a universally usable defence against abuse. This is not simply because its sources of inspiration, or at least of international assent, were anyway much broader than those summarised as liberalism, and extended to the tradition not only represented by Marx and various egalitarian social movements, but also to all of the world's ethical systems (Ishay, 1997). Nor is it simply because, when compared with the liberal record, these other traditions may be shown to have provided, for example, a more effective basis for the protection of labour. More profoundly, it is because this critique opens international human rights discourse to a wealth of locally and diversely generated insights as to how the abuse of human frailty might be reduced (Chan, 2002; Davis, 1995; Guttmann, 2001; Keown, 1998). In other words, it suggests a way in which the discourse may be saved from its possible fate as a fig leaf that excuses abusers of their responsibilities, and instead ensures that it becomes a more truly cosmopolitan means by which abusers may be held to account.

The more specific, and in a sense technical, argument of this book has been that there is a place for sociology amongst the discourses on human rights. More particularly, because its object of interest is social structure in all its variety, it has been argued that sociology has something to contribute to the solution of the problem of enforcement. The basic elaboration and institutionalisation of human rights within the UN as a putative global ethic has been an immensely complex project that has absorbed not only the energies of a very large number of people both within and outside the organisation, but has also required vast amounts of goodwill between nations. However, there are limits to what individual and organisational ingenuity and goodwill can achieve, as instanced by the social-structurally determined decision to re-write the Universal Declaration of Human Rights as two separate treaties, and by the geopolitically overdetermined silence within the discourse to which it gave birth about the power differences that mark the global social structure and that are indexed by the rise of the narrow form of the doctrine of justiciability.

This said, my argument has been that there is a need for still more ingenuity in the form of the development of a method for translating between the two covenants, especially since it is likely to foster the currently rather attenuated goodwill necessary to make further improvements in the effectiveness of human rights protections. The translations for which I have argued have been limited largely because, as indicated in the Preface and argued for in Chapter 4, the so-called civilisational dispute over human rights has a much more restricted scope than is commonly supposed in that, for example, the concerns of the more conservative Asian governments are rather narrowly focused on the freedoms of association and expression as opposed to human rights as such.

Now, although the labour rights upon which I have concentrated are amongst the principal sites of these concerns, they are not of course the only such sites, since similar sites exist across the whole range of human activity, and arise wherever individuals and governments have different views and interests. Thus my title may be seen to have a second meaning, in that making human rights work globally also involves making a lot more work for the human rights community. This said, my hope is that the present study provides at least the beginnings of some guidance as to the basis upon which this work should be carried out.

Thus the most general lessons I have derived from my labour rights case study are fourfold. Although they will no doubt be resisted by the more extreme neo-liberal human rights idolaters, they will seem blindingly obvious to many historians, political scientists and sociologists. First, as both Hohfeld and, very recently, O'Neill (2002, pp 28ff) have made clear, even in individualistic societies 'claims' are generally far more reliably enforced than 'liberties', since they impose duties on specific agencies or agents whereas the latter do not. Secondly, full recognition of economic and social rights is both easier to achieve than is supposed by neo-liberals (Arambulo, 1999; Craven, 1995; Hodgson, 1999; Hunt, 1996; Sen, 1999a; Toebes, 1999; Tomasevski, 1999), and can have a preventive effect in relation to the possibility of civil and political derogations. Thus if Northern governments are truly concerned about the civil and political rights of Southern citizens, they should give up their opposition to the right to development and accept the duties and obligations this would lay on them. Thirdly, legislative acceptance of demands for 'powers' and 'claims' is the best antidote to the disorderly expression of freedoms, as even the recent histories of struggles around 'race', gender and sexual orientation in the West make very clear. Equally obviously, although the passage of such legislation in Western Europe, if not the United States, owed something to the benevolence of paternalistic conservative governments, it owed a lot more to political pressure from below, so why should it be any different in the South (Langlois, 2001)? Fourthly, it should be recognised that liberties, including the freedoms of association and expression, do not flourish spontaneously but require nurturing, and so may often involve, as exemplified by the establishment of Labour Departments, establishing claims on the state—for example, in the form of access to human rights commissions, such as exist, however imperfectly and ineffectively, in Japan (Neary, 2002, Chapter 2), Mexico and Ghana (International Council on Human Rights Policy, 2000). In sum, then, it seems that liberty is only of critical importance in extreme situations, and that these occur most frequently where states refuse to recognise the legitimacy of their citizens' demands for state protection; that is, in either dictatorial or, ironically, ultra-liberal states.

American dominance and future of human rights

At the end of Chapter 4 I acknowledged that there was at least one serious problem with my argument, namely the possibility that translation might provide an excuse for regression. I now wish to acknowledge the existence of a second problem, which is that, given the global distribution of power, the successful implementation of the translation strategy depends upon the strategy gaining the support of the United States, which is simultaneously one of the most culturally distinctive societies in the world and the most influential within the current human rights regime. Thus it is the society that has the greatest reason to fear that it may be a loser if even the limited form of translation advocated here should become part of the methodology of human rights. To understand how the United States might respond to the possibility of such a development, one has to understand its relationship to globalisation, which, of course, is a highly complicated undertaking. However, given that this is a conclusion to a study of something else, a very brief sketch of this relationship and its implications for the problem at hand will have to suffice.

If one were to update the account of the discursive formation pertinent to human rights provided in Chapter 1 to take it from 1990 up to the end of the Clinton presidency, one would represent it as a clear continuation of the previous period. Thus Robertson's description of what he terms the 'Uncertainty Phase' in the history of globalisation (see above, p 23) would have remained broadly accurate, in that the United Nations continued to provide the principal site wherein the discourse of human rights was elaborated, Western nations and INGOs remained the principal authorities of delimitation, and their language, legal traditions and preference for civil and political over economic and social rights also remained dominant with respect to the style and conceptual content of the discourse. Finally, the energy, if not the consistency, with which the Clinton Administration invoked the goal of the protection of human rights as the touchstone of its foreign policy strongly suggests that the discourse retained its functionality as regards the United

States' geopolitical position. And this despite that Administration's deeply disappointing record as regards domestic rights protection, especially in the areas of racial discrimination in the criminal justice system, labour's freedoms of speech and association, aid to single parents, and health care. Moreover, some of the tensions that Robertson points to had become somewhat muted and the signs of the existence of a more authentically global polity rather more in evidence. This was largely the consequence of two developments: the normalising of the uni-polar international relations system created by the collapse of the Soviet Empire and the (temporary?) weakening of the Asian challenge to the resulting American dominance because of the financial crisis in that region.

What was heartening about what happened during the resulting period of relative calm was that the United States government appeared to have become more relaxed about its dominant role, in that it had seemed more prepared to allow more space to global institutions to evolve according to their own internal dynamics, in the economic realm at least. Thus, for example, the World Bank (1995) was able to produce a report that spoke favourably of the role of trade unions as contributors to equitable economic development; the World Trade Organization was able to reject the American-sponsored Social Clause as well as the Multinational Agreement on Investment (MAI), which would have greatly increased the powers of transnational corporations relative to nation states; and the International Monetary Fund (IMF) has been able to accept criticisms, from dissident American economists and the World Bank as well as governments, of its response to the Asian financial crisis as being insensitive to the social consequences of its support terms. Moreover, the Asian financial crisis itself provided an opportunity for a shared appreciation of where their common interests lie to develop between the United States and its most likely future challenger, China, as the latter resisted the temptation to devalue its currency and the former acknowledged the necessity of such co-operation.

None of this required one to deny that great dangers remained, especially on the political side. On the one hand, these were instanced by the festering anger and multiple resentments of the Islamic world. On the other, they were instanced by the United States' and Britain's apparent belief that they could unilaterally (that is, without UN approval) and with impunity launch attacks with planes and missiles on other nations (Libya, Sudan, Serbia, and Afghanistan even before the destruction of the World Trade Center), callously maintain a sanctions regime despite its demonstrable and disproportionate harm to the civilian population (Iraq), and compromise the legitimacy and effectiveness of UN inspection teams by, contrary to the terms of the pertinent UN resolutions, placing their intelligence agents within the teams (Iraq). 'Might makes right' is always a dangerous doctrine, no matter how apparently just the cause, and especially if both sides to a conflict adopt it as their strategy—as some 3,000 innocents discovered so horribly on September 11, 2001.

Although it is now incredibly hard to bracket these dangers, one nevertheless has to try if one wishes to think positively about the future. Thus what is presently so depressing is that the September 11 massacre appears to have confirmed the present American Administration in its prior rejection (Fitzgerald, 2002) of Clintonian pragmatism and, indeed, of any global strategy in any policy area other than 'America first'. The Clinton Administration's pragmatism was one that arose from an apparently increasingly acute sense of the world's complexity, and therefore of the need for its sophisticated management, if only to protect the interests of the United States. This was also a pragmatism that had deep roots, albeit within the context of the Cold War policy of containment, in that it had long been exemplified in the realm of political economy by various instances of power-sharing. Examples include encouraging European integration, sponsoring the development of the Asia Pacific Economic Conference (APEC), and looking kindly on the development of the Asia-Europe Meeting (ASEM).

For the time being at least, any hope that such pragmatism might be extended to include an appreciation of either the contribution made by American foreign policy failures to the dangerousness of the current world situation over many years (far too much inconsistency and carelessness with respect to what is currently termed 'collateral damage' in its use of violence and far too weak a commitment to eradicating the causes of the violent actions of others), or of the level of cultural sophistication that is required of the United States if it is to contribute to the global embedding of human rights. Both possibilities appear to have disappeared as a consequence of the Bush Administration's thinly disguised adoption of the policy conclusions that follow from the 'Clash of Civilisations' doctrine—or so it seems at first sight. Taking a second look, however, if one takes seriously the sociological premises upon which Huntington's policy conclusions rest, and as indeed he himself argues, it logically follows that the United States should allow other states to go their own ways on human rights. Moreover, many conservative politicians and thinkers already use an extreme and thoroughly relativist version of what might be termed the 'translation strategy', in the form of the well-established argument that the United States' ratification of the International Covenant on Economic, Social and Cultural Rights (ICESCR) is unnecessary, since in the 'homeland' economic and social rights are actualised through the supposedly universal and globally exemplary diffusion of civil and political capabilities. Most recently and most disturbingly, this same exemplary diffusion has been used to justify: the refusal to support the establishment of an International Criminal Court (ICC) that might have tried American citizens for war crimes; the refusal to sign the optional protocol to the Torture Convention that would have allowed international monitors into American gaols; the violation of the rights of the prisoners of war held at Camp Delta; and the dramatic weakening of *habeas corpus* that followed the tragedy of September 11.

Fortunately for the very large numbers of poor and powerless people in the United States (Edsall, 1984; Schwartz, 1997; Ehrenreich, 2001) and the rest of the world, and as I have endeavoured to show in the foregoing, neither international human rights discourse nor a properly sophisticated form of sociological reasoning supports so extreme a form of relativism. Nor, indeed, is it credible that in the longer term the United States' interests would be best served by the isolationism that informs it, particularly given China's significance as a potential catalyst of an alternative, Asian-centred world order. Nevertheless, and with an irony that bespeaks the status of globalisation and international human rights discourse as aspects of a 'total social fact', the processes set in train by the United States' neglect of the continuing functionality of human rights for the maintenance of America's global position might yet produce a situation in which the Bush Administration's adoption of an isolationist stance, informed by Huntingtonian relativism, could facilitate the acceptance of the much more limited translations for which I have argued as part of a new global human rights settlement. Not only would all the power previously invested by the United States in the human rights project not be returned to it, but also other forces could fill the vacuum left by any American withdrawal, and use the 'American power' that remains intrinsic to the project to change its character.

Were this to happen, it appears to me that the momentum behind any resulting change could well be considerable, in that it is likely to be enhanced by several other recent, and at first sight unconnected, events. First, the ICC has been established despite American disapproval and, although it has no jurisdiction over American citizens acting for their government, it may yet gain jurisdiction over them when they work for international organisations, notwithstanding Congress' recent passing of what has become known as the 'Hague Invasion Act'. Secondly, the principal Western human rights INGOs, Amnesty International and Human Rights Watch, are now both much more independent of governments than they once were, and they have begun to pay much closer attention to economic and social issues. Thirdly, despite the disappointing results so far of the 'Drop the Debt' campaigns and, most recently, of the Johannesburg Summit, recognition of the need to reduce global poverty has begun to influence Northern policy makers (edging towards accepting the right to development?). Fourthly, the normally ideologically unassertive Japanese government, which manages what is still the world's second biggest national economy, has recently begun to elaborate a distinctive vision which could provide the basis for a new global human rights settlement. This vision is what is called the 'human security approach', and it clearly insists both on the indivisibility of the two covenants and on the need to both take account of and respect social difference:

> Human security is an approach aimed at reinforcing measures to attach importance to the viewpoints of each individual so as to protect people from threats against subsistence, life and dignity and to realize the rich potential of each individual (Prime Minister Koizumi, quoted in the *Japan Times*, 16 December 2001).

> When people respect different values and opinions...they can coexist peacefully. Such attitudes help prevent conflicts and lead to promoting human security (Foreign Minister Tanaka, quoted in the *Japan Times*, 16 December 2001).

What, to my mind, makes these words particularly worthy of note are two of their perhaps less obvious implications. First, they, and the argument of mine they complete, suggest just how quickly American human rights exceptionalism could turn into global isolation and its righteousness into defensiveness—how easy would it be to argue that individual security is more important than human security, given that the latter includes the former? Secondly, there is the implication that follows from the fact that they were spoken by the leaders of the country that, by Western standards, has the best human rights record in Asia, and therefore they prompt the recollection of the high price the Japanese had to pay for this achievement. In the light of all the current appallingly easy talk of 'armed humanitarianism' (Douzinas, 2002), with its disturbing Bolshevik echoes, it is salutary to recall that it took many, many deaths, the dropping of two atomic bombs, a military occupation, a remarkably wide-ranging programme of social re-engineering, and extraordinary resilience and creativity on the part of the people, to make the Japanese achievement possible. Surely, no improvement in a country's human rights could ever justify the repetition of such a programme of action, or 'nation-building', as it would be called today. However, any military action that is not accompanied by such a programme is likely to result in simple 'regime change', and therefore to amount to little more than the gratuitous violence that is so transparently denied as 'collateral damage' and so carelessly forgotten when the manifestly self-serving notion, I will not call it a right, of 'pre-emptive self-defence' is invoked.

If the war on Iraq that seems so imminent at the time of writing actually occurs, it, and especially its aftermath, will have represented another equally awful social experiment, since we will finally find out if the term 'globalisation' is anything more than a reinvented form of imperialism, as some fear (Hardt and Negri, 2001), others desire (Cooper, 2002), and President Bush appears to affirm, when he attempts to justify 'pre-emptive self-defence' by referring to the necessity of preventing the emergence of a rival super-power. If the United States and Britain either win significant and willing global support, or cancel their threatened invasion given the lack of it, there will remain a chance that globalisation as defined above (see p 13) has become a reality in the sense that not even so massively dominant a super-power as the United States can act independently. If, however, they decide to go it alone despite the absence of significant global support, are victorious, find no weapons of mass destruction, and are not ostracised within the international system, we will know that a new imperium has been established, and that such cosmopolitan discourses as that articulated here will once again have to be subordinated to those of national liberation. And rightly so, since many amongst the world's population will have quite reasonably come to the conclusion that international human rights discourse has been so tainted by its association with this new imperium that it will only regain any credibility, let alone any protective power, once it has been rediscovered and reinvented within the context of the struggle against the same narcissistic empire. Whatever the outcome, it is clear that the ultimate threat to American dominance is most likely to come not from a rival super-power but from the wider world in all its resistant particularity—*vive la differénce.*

Postscript: 10 May 2003

Sadly, my worst case scenario appears to be the one that is being enacted. Uncounted thousands of often unwilling Iraqi soldiers and hundreds of civilians have been killed in the prosecution of an illegal and globally unsupported war. Also, and as if to confirm the world's disquiet, the 'liberation' of Baghdad was marked by ambiguous responses on the part of 'liberators' and 'liberated' alike. In an extraordinary 'Freudian slip' that was broadcast to the world, the 'liberating' American marines initially draped the 'stars and stripes' rather than the Iraqi flag over Saddam Hussein's head as they worked to topple his statue. Similarly, the 'liberated' engaged in only the most muted of celebrations, during which hatred of the former dictator was far more obvious than gratitude to those who had removed him. Thus another war fought in the name of the American version of human rights or, as one marine evocatively put it whilst trying to hold back a protesting crowd, 'your fucking freedom', has again been met with a mixture of scepticism and/or hostility. What is more, the resulting occupation has also, and remarkably quickly, been challenged by passionately expressed ethnically, regionally and religiously inflected patriotisms that, for the time being at least, explicitly prioritise very different human rights from those summarised by the term 'freedom', namely those of an adequate standard of living, national self-determination and religious freedom.

The differences between the 'liberators' and the 'liberated' are therefore far sharper than those I had in mind as I developed the translation strategy outlined above. Moreover, one can expect the intensification and repetition of such differences as other self-defined humanitarianisms take up arms in order to pre-empt attacks by the new imperial legions. This is especially the case given that these legions are permanently primed to attack by a doctrine of imminent danger that is even more subjective than that of 'clear and present danger' developed by the American Supreme Court to deal with the threat posed by domestic communists at the height of the Cold War. This new imperial project is, however, more than normally hubristic since, in my judgment, it has already been made impossible by the inadequacy of the means available in relation to the magnitude of the task: the other globally broadcast set of images that the world will never forget was that of the United States' Secretary of State, Colin Powell, losing the debate in the UN Security Council. Given globalisatipn and the representative structures, procedural rules-and, now, global visibility it has brought to the international system, policies and arguments are now much more likely to be judged on their merits than in the past—no wonder the Bush Administration is now so intent on avoiding 'entanglements' with the the UN in the future. However, military might alone, no matter how effectively deployed, will not be enough to deliver —let alone sustain—an empire, not just because it never is enough, but also because the United States, as the biggest and indeed most indebted global player, is necessarily more dependent on the co-operation of others than any other state. Thus China, thanks to North Korea, was not even threatened with punishment for its failure to join the 'coalition of the willing', whilst the punishment promised for Germany, France, Russia and Turkey in relation to the same failure is most likely either to come to nothing or to rebound on the United States because the support of the previously unwilling is required for other projects—vassals who escape punishment typically lose their fear, become unreliable and strike hard bargains, witness Magna Carta.

Traumatised by the attack of September 11 and having as a result, contrarily and imprudently, decided to go for victory in what it supposes to be a clash of civilisations, the present American Administration can be expected to resist vigorously any efforts to, as the Administration would no doubt put it, weaken the prerogatives of freedom and so further undermine the United States' claims to global moral superiority. That said, the emboldened vassals may soon find it to be in their interests to take a more explicitly cosmopolitan line in reshaping the discourse that the Magna Carta initiated. If they do follow such a course, their motives are unlikely to be any purer than those of the Barons who confronted the king at Runnymede but, given the power now inherent in international human rights discourse, their actions too may nevertheless produce benefits for those people throughout the world who are vulnerable to abuse. In the meantime, making human rights work globally has become both even more important if we are to avoid a descent into barbarism, and even harder because of the degree to which this descent has already occurred. Moreover, the situation is now so dangerous that neither ingenuity nor the power inherent in the global human rights system is likely to be enough to prevent this descent continuing. Ridiculous as it may seem to the *soi-disant* sophisticates who rule the world, hard-headed, altruistic idealism rather than easy, macho realism is what is currently required in the international system, and especially of those who, ignorant—or worse—careless of the malevolent Kafkaesque/Orwellian connotations of such impersonal euphemisms, have chosen to call their apparatus of occupation in Iraq the 'Authority'.

Appendix
The interview schedules

All of the workplace interviewees were asked the following questions:

(1) How long have you been a member of this company?
(2) Is this your first industrial job? If not, for what sort of company and in what position did you work before?
(3) What is your present job title and how long is your present contract for? Please describe the nature of the work you do.
(4) If you have a technical problem with your work such as...(will depend on position)..., would you try to solve it yourself or would you seek help from someone else?

(5) If someone else, would they most likely be:

  (a) a fellow worker?
  (b) your work group?
  (c) a supervisor?
  (d) a manager?
  (e) a trade union official?
  (f) none of the above?

(6) Please explain why you would turn to such a person.
(7) If you cannot resolve the problem with this advice, what would you do next?
(8) If you have a problem with a colleague, who for example is bullying you, would you try to solve it yourself or seek help from someone else?
(9) If someone else, would they most likely be:

  (a) a fellow worker?
  (b) your work group?
  (c) a supervisor?
  (d) a manager?
  (e) a trade union official?
  (f) none of the above?

(10) Please explain why you would turn to such a person.

(11) Since you started working here, have you ever consulted your employment contract?

(12) If so and without giving us any confidential details, can you tell us:

(a) why?
(b) if and in what way it was helpful?

(13) If you have a personal problem of any kind, say a family problem, which is not connected with your work, is there anyone in the company you would discuss it with?

(14) Is that person:

(a) a colleague?
(b) a supervisor?
(c) a trade union official?
(d) a manager?

(15) Do you think that the company should help you with problems that are not their contractual responsibility?

(16) Are there any differences in the way you would go about solving any of the problems we have discussed in this company when compared with the way you solved them in your previous employment?

(17) Have you ever taken any sort of problem to any one or more of the following:

(a) a supervisor?
(b) a manager?
(c) a trade union official?
(d) a mediator?
(e) an arbitrator?
(f) a judge?

(18) Without telling us anything about the problem itself, can you tell us if you were happy with the result?

(19) If you felt that someone in a higher position than you in the company was treating you unfairly, would you tell them directly? Would you also think of telling another official in the company? Why or why not?

Supervisors, trade union officials and managers were asked these additional questions:

(20) What is your view of staff bringing their problems to you? Do you encourage, discourage, or neither encourage nor discourage them to do so? What are the reasons for your view?

(21) What sort of problems do your staff bring to you? Why do you think they bring them to you? Is it just because of your position or for some other reason? If for some other reason, what is it?

(22) Do you ever think that they need not have troubled you?

(23) Without telling us what it was about, have any of your subordinates ever complained about your decisions or behaviour, no matter how unreasonably?

The arbitrators were asked the following questions:

(1) What are the two or three most common types of work-related problems you have to deal with? For each of these, how do you typically go about trying to solve them?
(2) Is the employment contract ever helpful to you in trying to find a solution? If so, please tell us in what ways it is useful.
(3) Are administrative manuals, legislation or legal decisions ever helpful to you in trying to find a solution? If so, please tell us in what ways each of them is useful.
(4) Do you ever consult trade union or other Labour Bureau officials?
(5) Is common sense sometimes more useful than any other resource in trying to solve these problems? If so, what sort of ideas does it involve?
(6) Do you have any strong ideas about the duties of managers in relation to their staff ? For example, do you think that they should be prepared to help them with non-work related problems if they can or does their responsibility end at the factory gates?
(7) Do you think that many of the problems you have had to deal with really should not have been brought to you?
(8) Without giving away any confidential details, what are the most difficult types of cases you have had to deal with?

Bibliography

Abel, RL (ed) (1982) *The Politics of Informal Justice,* New York: Academic Press

Abrahamson, B and Brostrom, A (1980) *The Rights of Labor,* Beverley Hills: Sage

Adamic, L (1963) *Dynamite: The History of Class Violence in the United States,* Gloucester, Mass: P Smith

Ago, S (1995) 'The social clause as understood in Asia', mimeo, Kyushu University, Faculty of Law

Alston, P (1992) 'The Committee on Economic, Social and Cultural Rights', in Alston, P (ed) (1992) *The United Nations and Human Rights: A Critical Appraisal* Oxford: OUP

Alston, P and Crawford, J (eds) (2000) *The Future of United Nations Human Rights Treaty Monitoring,* Cambridge: CUP

An-Na'im, AA (1990) *Toward an Islamic Reformation: Civil Liberties, Human Rights and International Law,* Syracuse: Syracuse UP

Arambulo, K (1999) *Strengthening the Supervision of the International Covenant on Economic, Social and Cultural Rights,* Oxford: Intersentia-Hart

Archibugi, D, Held, D and Kohler, M (eds) (1998) *Re-imagining Political Community: Studies in Cosmopolitan Democracy,* Cambridge: Polity

Atsushi, H (1995) 'Overseas Japanese plants under global strategies: TV transplants in Asia', in Frenkel, S and Harrod, J (eds) (1995) *Industrialization and Labor Relations: Contemporary Research in Seven Countries,* Ithaca: ILR Press

Badiou, A (2001) *Ethics: An Essay on the Understanding of Evil,* London: Verso

Bales, K (1999) *Disposable People: New Slavery in the Global Economy,* Berkeley: University of California Press

Bao, L (1998) 'Work: questions and answers' 31(6) Chinese Law and Government 70–96

Barber, B (1995) *Jihad versus McWorld,* New York: Times Books

Bataille, G (1973) *Theory of Religion,* New York: Zone Books

Bauer, J (2000) 'Human rights for all? The problem of the human rights box', Human Rights Dialogue, series 2, no 1 , 1–3

Bauer, J and Bell, D (eds) (1999) *The East Asian Challenge for Human Rights,* Cambridge: CUP

Be, J (1996) 'Mediation, arbitration and litigation: dispute resolution in the People's Republic of China' 15(1) UCLA Pacific Basin LJ 122–37

Beetham, D (1998) 'Human rights as a model for cosmopolitan democracy', in Archibugi, D, Held, D and Kohler, M (eds) (1998) *Re-imagining Political Community: Studies in Cosmopolitan Democracy,* Cambridge: Polity

Bennett, J and Ishino, I (1972) *Paternalism in the Japanese Economy,* Westport: Greenwood

Benton, T (1993) *Natural Relations: Ecology, Animal Rights and Social Justice,* London: Verso

Berlin, I (1969) *Four Essays on Liberty,* Oxford: OUP

Bhabha, H (1994) *The Location of Culture,* London: Routledge

Bhagwati, J and Hudec, R (eds) (1996) *Fair Trade and Harmonisation: Prerequisites for Free Trade,* vol 2, Cambridge: MIT Press

Blackstone, Sir William, *Commentaries on the Laws of England,* Morrison, W (ed) (2001) London: Cavendish Publishing

Bradshaw, Y and Wallace, M (1996) *Global Inequalities,* Thousand Oaks: Pine Forge Press

Broadhurst, R (ed) (1999) *Crime and Indigenous Justice,* Special Issue, 32(1) Australia and New Zealand Journal of Criminology

Burchell, G and Gordon, C (eds) (1991) *The Foucault Effect: Studies in Governmentality,* London: Harvester Wheatsheaf

Campbell, T, Ewing, K and Tomkins, A (2001) *Sceptical Essays on Human Rights,* Oxford: OUP

Cassese, A (1990) *Human Rights in a Changing World,* Oxford: Polity

Chan, A (1994) 'Revolution or corporatism: worker in search of a solution', in Goodman, D and Hooper, B (eds) (1994) *China's Quiet Revolution,* Melbourne: Longman Cheshire

Chan, A (1998a) 'Labor standards and human rights: the case of Chinese workers under market socialism' 20(4) Human Rights Quarterly 886–904

Chan, A (ed) (1998b) 'The conditions of Chinese workers in Asian-funded enterprises' 30(4) Chinese Sociology and Anthropology 3–101

Chan, J (2002) 'Moral autonomy, civil liberties and Confucianism' 52(2) Philosophy East and West

Charnovitz, S (1987) 'The influence of international labor standards on the world trading regimes: a historical overview' 126(5) International Labour Review 565–84

Chatterjee, P (1998) 'Community in the East', Economic and Political Weekly, 7 February, 277–82

Chen, AH-Y (1998) *An Introduction to the Legal System of the People's Republic of China,* Hong Kong: Butterworths Asia

Cohen, S (2000) *States of Denial: Knowing About Atrocities and Suffering,* Oxford: Blackwell

Compa, L and Diamond, S (eds) (1996) *Human Rights, Labor Rights and International Trade,* Philadephia: University of Pennsylvania Press

Cooper, R (2002) 'Why we still need empires', in Foreign Policy Centre (2002), *Reordering the World,* London

Craib, I (1998) *Experiencing Identity,* London: Sage

Craven, M (1995) *The International Covenant on Economic, Social and Cultural Rights,* Oxford: OUP

Davis, MC (ed) (1995) *Human Rights and Chinese Values,* New York: OUP

de Sousa Santos, B (1995) *Toward a New Common-sense: Law, Politics and Science in the Paradigmatic Transition,* New York: Routledge

Donnelly, J (1989) *Universal Human Rights in Theory and Practice,* Ithaca: Cornell UP

Douzinas, C (2000) *The End of Human Rights,* Oxford: Hart

Douzinas, C (2002) 'Postmodern just wars: Kosovo, Afghanistan and the new world order', in Strawson, J (ed) (2002) *Law after Ground Zero,* London: GlassHouse Press

Durkheim, E (1895) *The Rules of Sociological Method,* reprinted 1982, Basingstoke: Macmillan

Dworkin, R (2002) 'The threat to patriotism', *New York Review of Books* 28

Edelman, B (1979) *Ownership of the Image,* London: Routledge

Edsall, T (1984) *The New Politics of Inequality,* New York: Norton

Ehrenberg, R (ed) (1994) *Labor Markets and Integrating National Economies,* Washington: The Brookings Institution

Ehrenreich, B (2001) *Nickel and Dimed: On (not) Getting By in America,* New York: Metropolitan Books

Evans, P (1995) *Embedded Autonomy: States and Industrial Transformation,* Princeton: Princeton UP

Evans, T (1996) *US Hegemony and the Project of Universal Human Rights,* Basingstoke: Macmillan

Ewing, K (1994) *Britain and the ILO,* 2nd edn, London: Institute of Employment Rights

Featherstone, M (ed) (1990) *Global Culture: Nationalism, Globalisaton and Modernity,* London: Sage

Featherstone, M (1995) *Undoing Culture: Globalization, Postmodernism and Identity,* London: Sage

Featherstone, M, Lash, S and Robertson, R (eds) (1995) *Global Modernities,* London: Sage

Fisher, D and Harris, L (1983) *The Right to Communicate: A New Human Right,* Dublin: Boole

Flood, PJ (1998) *The Effectiveness of UN Human Rights Institutions,* Westport, Conn: Praeger

Foreign Policy Centre (2002) *Reordering the World,* London

Foucault, M (1972) *The Archaeology of Knowledge,* London: Tavistock

Frank, T (2000) *One Market under God: Extreme Capitalism, Market Populism and the End of Economic Democracy,* New York: Doubleday

Freeman, R (1994) 'Comments', in Ehrenberg, R (ed) (1994) *Labor Markets and Integrating National Economies,* Washington: The Brookings Institution

Frenkel, S and Harrod, J (eds) (1995) *Industrialization and Labor Relations: Contemporary Research in Seven Countries,* Ithaca, NY: ILR Press

Fukuyama, F (1982) *The End of History and the Last Man,* New York: Free Press.

Gaete, R (1993) *Human Rights and the Limits of Critical Reason,* Aldershot: Dartmouth

Garon, S (1987) *The State and Labor in Japan,* Berkeley: University of California Press

Garon, S (1999) 'Collective labor law in Japan since 1882', in van der Linden, M and Price, R (eds) (1999) *The Rise and Development of Collective Labour Law,* Berne: Peter Lang

Gergen, K (1991) *The Saturated Self,* New York: Basic Books

Gibbons, S (1998) *International Labour Rights—New Methods of Enforcement,* London: Institute of Employment Rights

Giddens, A (1990) *The Consequences of Modernity,* Palo Alto, CA: Stanford UP

Gilroy, P (1994) *The Black Atlantic: Modernity and Double Consciousness,* London: Verso

Golub, S (1997) 'International labor standards and international trade', mimeo, Washington: IMF

Goodman, D and Hooper, B (eds) (1994) *China's Quiet Revolution,* Melbourne: Longman Cheshire

Gould, W (2000) *Labored Relations: Law, Politics and the NLRB,* Cambridge, Mass: MIT Press

Guthrie, D (1999) *The Dragon in a Three-Piece Suit: the Emergence of Capitalism in China,* Princeton: Princeton UP

Guttman, A (2001) 'Introduction', in Ignatieff, M (2001) *Human Rights as Politics and Idolatry,* Princeton: Princeton UP

Hall, S and Du Gay, P (eds) (1996) *Questions of Cultural Identity,* London: Sage

Halliday, F (1994) *Rethinking International Relations,* Basingstoke: Macmillan

Halpin, A (1997) *Rights and Law, Analysis and Theory,* Oxford: Hart

Hamelink, C (1994) *The Politics of World Communication: A Human Rights Perspective,* London: Sage

Hannum, H (ed) (1992) *Guide to International Human Rights Practice,* 2nd edn, Philadelphia: University of Pennsylvania Press

Hannum, H and Fischer, D (eds) (1993) *US Ratification of the International Covenants on Human Rights,* New York: Transnational

Hardt, M and Negri, A (2001) *Empire,* Cambridge, Mass: Harvard UP

Harrod, J (1987) *Power, Production and the Unprotected Workers,* New York: Columbia UP

Hayner, PB (2001) *Unspeakable Truths,* New York: Routledge

Hepple, B (ed) (1986) *The Making of Labour Law in Europe,* London: Mansell

Hickson, D (ed) (1993) *Management in Western Europe: Society, Culture and Organisation in Twelve Nations,* Berlin: de Gruyter

Hirschman, AO (1970) *Exit, Voice and Loyalty: Responses to Decline in Organizations, Firms and States,* Cambridge, Mass: Harvard UP

Hirst, P (1979) *On Law and Ideology,* London: Macmillan

Hodgson, D (1999) *The Human Right to Education,* Aldershot: Dartmouth

Hohfeld, W (1919) *Fundamental Legal Conceptions as Applied to Judicial Reasoning, and Other Legal Essays,* New Haven: Yale UP

Hughes, S and Wilkinson, R (1998) 'International labour standards and world trade: no role for the World Trade Oganization?' 3(3) New Political Economy 375–89

Human Rights Watch (2000) *Unfair Advantage: Workers' Freedom of Association in the United States,* New York

Hunt, P (ed) (1996) *Reclaiming Social Rights,* Aldershot: Dartmouth

Ignatieff, M (2001) *Human Rights as Politics and Idolatry,* Princeton: Princeton UP

International Council on Human Rights Policy (2000) *Performance and Legitimacy: National Human Rights Institutions,* Geneva

Ishay, M (1997) *The Human Rights Reader,* New York: Routledge

Isin, E and Turner, B (2002) *A Handbook of Citizenship Studies,* London: Sage

Jabine, T and Claude, R (eds) (1992) *Human Rights and Statistics,* Philadelphia: University of Pennsylvania Press

Jackson, R (1990) *Quasi-States: Sovereignty, International Relations and the Third World,* Cambridge: CUP

Jacobs, A (1986) 'Collective self-regulation', in Hepple, B (ed) (1986) *The Making of Labour Law in Europe,* London: Mansell

Jacoby, S (1997) *Modern Manors: Welfare Capitalism since the New Deal,* Princeton: Princeton UP

Jenkins, R (1996) *Social Identity,* London: Routledge

Jessop, B (1990) *State Theory,* Cambridge: Polity

Johnston, GA (1970) *The International Labour Organisation: Its Work for Social and Economic Progress,* London: Europa

Jones, K (1982) *Law and Economy,* Toronto: Academic Press

Josephs, H (1990) *Labor Law in China: Choice and Responsibility,* Salem: Butterworths

Josephs, H (1995) 'Labor law in a "socialist market economy": the case of China' 23(3) Columbia Journal of Transnational Law 559–81

Kahn-Freund, O (1944) 'The illegality of a trade union' 7 Modern Law Review 192

Kahn-Freund, O (1977) *Labour and the Law,* 2nd edn, London: Stevens

Kahn-Freund, O (1981) *Labour Law and Politics in the Weimar Republic,* Oxford: Blackwell

Kaple, D (1994) *Dream of a Red Factory: The Legacy of High Stalinism in Russia,* New York: OUP

Keith, RC (1994) *China's Struggle for the Rule of Law,* Basingstoke: Macmillan

Kelly, D (1998) *Asian Freedoms,* Cambridge: CUP

Kent, A (1993) *Between Freedom and Subsistence: China and Human Rights,* Hong Kong: OUP

Kent, A (1999) *China, the United Nations, and Human Rights,* Philadelphia: University of Pennsylvania Press

Keown, D (ed) (1998) *Buddhism and Human Rights,* Richmond, Surrey: Curzon

Kettler, D and Tackney, C (1997) 'Light from a dead sun: the Japanese lifetime employment system and Weimar labor law' 19(1) Comparative Labour Law and Policy Journal

Klug, F (2000) *Values for a Godless Age,* Harmondsworth: Penguin

Kluver, A (1996) *Legitimating the Chinese Economic Reforms: A Rhetoric of Myth and Orthodoxy,* Albany: SUNY Press

Koh, T and van der Linden, M (2000) *Labour Relations in Asia and Europe,* Singapore: ASEF

Krugman, P (1997) 'What should trade negotiators negotiate about?' 35 Journal of Economic Literature 113–20

Langlois, A (2001) *The Politics of Justice and Human Rights: Southeast Asia and Universalist Theory,* Cambridge: CUP

Lash, S and Urry, J (1994) *Economy of Signs and Space,* London: Sage

Lauffs, A (ed) (1995) *China Update: The PRC Labour Law,* Hong Kong: Asia Law and Practice Publishing

Lauffs, A (ed) (1997) *China Staff Employment Manual,* Hong Kong: Asia Law and Practice Publishing

Lauren, PG (1998) *The Evolution of International Human Rights: Visions Seen,* Philadelphia: University of Pennsylvania Press

Lavender, S (1997) 'Labour unions', in Lauffs, A (ed) (1997) *China Staff Employment Manual,* Hong Kong: Asia Law and Practice Publishing

Leader, S (1992) *Freedom of Association: A Study of Labor Law and Political Theory,* New Haven: Yale UP

Leary, V (1996) 'The paradox of workers' rights as human rights', in Compa, L and Diamond, S (eds) (1996) *Human Rights, Labor Rights and International Trade,* Philadelphia: University of Pennsylvania Press

Lee, C (1998) 'Labor rights, globalization and an emerging issue—the Korean case', mimeo, Korea Labor Institute

Lee, C-K (1998) *Gender and the South China Miracle: Two Worlds of Factory Women,* Berkeley: University of California Press

Lee, E (1997) 'Globalization and labour standards: a review of the issues' 136(2) International Labour Rev 173–89

Leung, TW-Y (1988) *Smashing the Iron Rice Pot: Unions and Workers in China's Market Socialism,* Hong Kong: Asia Monitor Resource Centre

Leung, TW-Y (1998) 'The politics of labour rebellions in China, 1989–1994', unpublished PhD thesis, Department of Politics, Hong Kong University, Hong Kong

Levine, MJ (1997) *Worker Rights and Labor Standards in Asia's Four New Tigers: A Comparative Perspective,* New York: Plenum Press

Li, B-Y (1997) 'Rule of law in China: ideal and reality' 3(1) Journal of Chinese and Comparative Law 47–59

Li, H-L and Wang, Q (1996) *Research on the Chinese Work Unit Society,* Frankfurt: Lang

Lieberman, E (1950) *Unions Before the Bar,* New York: Harper

Lijnzaad, P (1995) *Reservations to United Nations Human Rights Treaties,* Dordrecht: Martinus Nijhoff

Liou, C (1993) 'The influences of foreign laws on the contemporary union rights policies in Taiwan', mimeo, Tokyo: Japan Institute of Labor

Logan, J, Bian, Y and Bian, F (1999) 'Housing inequality in China in the 1990s' 23(1) International Journal of Urban and Regional Research 17–25

Luard, E (1982) *A History of the United Nations,* Basingstoke: Macmillan

Luard, E (1989) *A History of the United Nations,* Basingstoke: Macmillan

Lukes, S (2001) Is there an alternative to market utopianism?', in Steiner, H and

Alston, P (2001) *International Human Rights in Context: Law, Politics, Morals,* Oxford: OUP

Mann, M (1986) *The Sources of Social Power,* vol 1, Cambridge: CUP

Mann, M (1993) 'Nation states in Europe and other continents: diversifying, developing, not dying', Daedalus, Winter, 115–40

Marks, S (2000) *The Riddle of All Constitutions,* Oxford: OUP

Marshall, TH (1949) 'Citizenship and social class', in Turner, B and Hamilton (eds) (1994) *Citizenship: Critical Concepts,* London: Routledge

Mauss, M (1924) *The Gift: the Form and Reason for Exchange in Archaic Societies,* reprinted 1990, London: Routledge

McGoldrick, D (1991) *The Human Rights Committee,* Oxford: OUP

Mehmet, O, Mendes, E and Sinding, R (1999) *Towards a Fair Global Market: Avoiding a New Slave Trade,* London: Routledge

Mehra, A (1986) *Free Flow of Communications: A New Paradigm,* New York: Greenwood

Merrils, J (1988) *The Development of International Law by the European Court of Human Rights,* Manchester: Manchester UP

Mills, K (1998) *Human Rights in the Emerging Global Order,* Basingstoke: Macmillan

Moore, M (2001) *Stupid White Men,* New York: Regan Books

Morsink, J (1999) *The Universal Declaration of Human Rights: Origins, Drafting and Intent,* Philadephia: University of Pennsylvania Press

Murphy, C (1994) *International Organization and Industrial Change,* Cambridge: Polity

Muzaffar, C (1993) *Human Rights and the New World Order,* Penang: Just World Trust

Neary, I (2002) *Human Rights in Japan, South Korea and Taiwan,* London: Routledge

Ng, S-K and Warner, M (1998) *China's Trade Unions and Management,* Basingstoke: Macmillan

Odinkalu, CA (2000) 'Why more Africans don't use human rights language', Human Rights Dialogue, series 2, no 1, 3–4

OECD (1996) *Trade Employment and Labour Standards: A Study of Core Workers' Rights and International Trade,* Paris: OECD

Olszak, N, 'The historical development of collective labour law: France', in van der Linden, M, and Price, R (eds) (1999) *The Rise and Development of Collective Labour Law,* Berne: Peter Lang

O'Neill, O (2002) *A Question of Trust,* Cambridge: CUP

Ong, K and Baxter, C (1999) 'A comparative study of the fundamental elements of Chinese and English property law' 48(1) International and Comparative Law Quarterly 88–126

Orren, K (1991) *Belated Feudalism: Labor, the Law, and Liberal Development,* Cambridge: CUP

Osieke, E (1985) *Constitutional Law and the Practice in the International Labour Organisation,* Dordrecht: Martinus Nijhoff

Pereira, W (1997) *InHuman Rights: The Western System and Global Human Rights Abuse,* Mapusa: The Other India Press

Putterman, L (1996) 'The role of ownership and property rights in China's economic transition', in Walder, A (1996) *China's Transitional Economy,* Oxford: OUP

Puttnam, R (2000) *Bowling Alone: The Collapse and Revival of American Community,* New York: Simon and Schuster

Ramm, T (1986) 'Workers' participation, the representation of labour and special labour courts', in Hepple, B (ed) (1986) *The Making of Labour Law in Europe,* London: Mansell

Ramos, E (1990) *Dualistic Unionism and Industrial Relations,* Quezon City: New Day Publishers

Rancharan, BG (1997) *The Principle of Legality in International Human Rights Institutions,* The Hague: Martinus Nijhoff

Rawls, J (1999) *The Law of Peoples,* Cambridge, Mass: Harvard UP

Ren, X (1997) *Tradition of the Law and the Law of Tradition: Law, State and Social Control in China,* Westport: Greenwood

Renner, K (1949) *The Institutions of the Private Law and their Social Functions,* London: Routledge

Robertson, R (1990) 'Mapping the global condition: globalisation as the central concept', in Featherstone, M (ed) (1990) *Global Culture: Nationalism, Globalisaton and Modernity,* London: Sage

Rodrik, D (1995) 'Labor standards and international trade: moving beyond the rhetoric', mimeo, Washington: Overseas Development Council

Rouner, L (1988) *Human Rights and the World's Religions,* Notre Dame: University of Notre Dame Press

Ruccio, D, Resnick, S and Wolff, R (1991) 'Class beyond the nation state', Capital and Class, no 43, 25–41

Rucker, B (1968) *First Freedom,* Carbondale: Southern Illinois UP

Said, E (1993) *Culture and Imperialism,* London: Chatto and Windus

Salgardo, G (1999) 'Early retirement in Japan: the loss of a privileged citizenship?', unpublished PhD thesis, Department of Sociology, Essex University

Sartorius, R (ed) (1983) *Paternalism,* Minneapolis: University of Minnesota Press

Schneiderman, D (2000) 'Investment rules and the new constitutionalism' 25(3) Law and Social Inquiry 757–87

Schregle, J (1993) 'Dismissal protection in Japan' 132(4) International Labour Rev

Schwartz, J (1997) *The Illusion of Opportunity,* New York: WW Norton

Sellars, K (2002) *The Rise and Rise of Human Rights,* Stroud: Sutton Publishing

Sen, A (1999a) 'Human rights and economic achievements', in Bauer, J and Bell, D (eds) (1999) *The East Asian Challenge for Human Rights,* Cambridge: CUP

Sen, A (1999b) *Development as Freedom,* Oxford: OUP

Serres, M (1995) *Genesis,* Ann Arbor: University of Michigan Press

Servais, JM (1986) 'Flexibility and rigidity in international labour standards' 125(2) International Labour Rev 193–208

Sheehan, J (1998) *Chinese Workers: A New History,* London: Routledge

Shih, C-Y (1999) *Collective Democracy: Political and Legal Reform in China,* Hong Kong: Chinese UP

Shue, H (1980) *Basic Rights: Subsistence, Affluence, and US Foreign Policy,* Princeton: Princeton UP

Sohn, L (1994) *Rights in Conflict: The United Nations and South Africa,* New York: Transnational

Solinger, D (1999) 'Human rights issues in China's internal migration: insights from comparisons with Germany and Japan', in Bauer, J and Bell, D (eds) (1999) *The East Asian Challenge for Human Rights,* Cambridge: CUP

Solinger, D (1999) *Contesting Citizenship in Urban China,* Berkeley: University of California Press

Steiner, H and Alston, P (1996–2001), *International Human Rights in Context: Law, Politics, Morals,* Oxford: OUP

Steinfeld, E (1998) *Forging Reform in China: The Fate of State-owned Industry,* Cambridge: CUP

Stephens, J (1979) *The Transition from Capitalism to Socialism,* London: Macmillan

Stone, K (1999) 'Labor and the American State: the evolution of labor law in the United States', in van der Linden, M and Price, R (eds) (1999) *The Rise and Development of Collective Labour Law,* Berne: Peter Lang

Strawson, J (ed) (2002) *Law after Ground Zero,* London: GlassHouse Press

Sugeno, K (1992) *Japanese Labor Law,* Seattle: University of Washington Press

Summers, C and Grodin, J (1993) 'Article 7—Right to just and favourable conditions at work', in Hannum, H and Fischer, D (eds) (1993) *US Ratification of the International Covenants on Human Rights,* New York: Transnational

Swepston, L (1992) 'Human rights complaint procedures of the international labour organisation' , in Hannum, H (ed) (1992) *Guide to International Human Rights Practice,* 2nd edn, Philadelphia: University of Pennsylvania Press

Talbot, R (2002) 'The balancing act: counter-terrorism and civil liberties in British anti-terrorism law', in Strawson, J (ed) (2002) *Law after Ground Zero,* London: GlassHouse Press

Tang, J (ed) (1995) *Human Rights and International Relations in the Asia-Pacific Region,* London: Pinter

Taylor, C (1999) 'Conditions of an unforced consensus on human rights', in Bauer, J and Bell, D (eds) (1999) *The East Asian Challenge for Human Rights,* Cambridge: CUP

Toebes, B (1999) *The Right to Health as Human Right in International Law,* Oxford: Intersentia-Hart

Tolley, H (1987) *The United Nations Commission on Human Rights,* Boulder: Westview

Tomasevski, K (ed) (1999) *The Right to Food,* Dordrecht: Martinus Nijhoff

Turner, B and Hamilton, P (eds) (1994) *Citizenship: Critical Concepts,* London: Routledge

Turner, BS (1993) 'Outline of a theory of human rights' 27(3) Sociology 489–512

Twine, F (1994) *Citizenship and Social Rights,* London: Sage

Unger, R (1976) *Law in Modern Society*, New York: Free Press

van Beuren, G (1995) *The International Law on the Rights of the Child*, Dordrecht: Martinus Nijhoff

van der Linden, M and Price, R (eds) (1999) *The Rise and Development of Collective Labour Law*, Berne: Peter Lang

van Genugten, W and Perez-Bustillo, C (2001) *The Poverty of Rights: Human Rights and the Eradication of Poverty*, London: Zed

Vincent, J (1986) *Human Rights and International Relations*, Cambridge: CUP

Walder, A (1986) *Communist Neo-Traditionalism*, Berkeley: University of California Press

Walder, A (1994) 'Evolving property rights and their political consequences', in Goodman, D and Hooper, B (eds) (1994) *China's Quiet Revolution*, Melbourne: Longman Cheshire

Walder, A (1996) *China's Transitional Economy*, Oxford: OUP

Walder, A (ed) (1998) *Zouping in Transition: The Process of Reform in Rural North China*, Cambridge, Mass: Harvard UP

Warner, M (1995) *The Management of Human Resources in Chinese Industry*, Basingstoke: Macmillan

Weatherly, R (1999) *The Discourse of Human Rights in China*, Basingstoke: Macmillan

Weber, M (1978) *Economy and Society*, 2 vols, Berkeley: University of California Press

Weiler, P (1990) *Governing the Workplace: The Future of Labor and Employment Law*, Cambridge, Mass: Harvard UP

Wellman, K (1989) 'A new conception of human rights', in Winston, M (ed) (1989) *The Philosophy of Human Rights*, Belmont: Wadsworth

Wilkinson, R and Hughes, S (1999) 'Labor standards and global governance: examining the dimensions of institutional engagement', mimeo, Department of Government, Manchester University

Wilkinson, R (1999) 'Labour and trade-related regulation: beyond the trade-labour standards debate?' 1(2) British Journal of Politics and International Relations 165–91

Wilson, R (ed) (1996) *Human Rights, Culture and Context*, London: Pluto

Wilson, R (2000) *The Politics of Truth and Reconciliation in South Africa*, Cambridge: CUP

Winston, M (ed) (1989) *The Philosophy of Human Rights*, Belmont: Wadsworth

Woodiwiss, A (1990a) *Social Theory After Postmodernism: Rethinking Production, Law and Class*, London: Pluto

Woodiwiss, A (1990b) *Rights v Conspiracy: A Sociological Essay on the Development of Labour Law in the United States*, Oxford: Berg

Woodiwiss, A (1992) *Law, Labour and Society in Japan: From Repression to Reluctant Recognition*, London: Routledge

Woodiwiss, A (1997) 'Against modernity: a dissident rant' 26(1) Economy and Society 1–21

Woodiwiss, A (1998) *Globalisation, Human Rights and Labour Law in Pacific Asia*, Cambridge: CUP

Woodiwiss, A (1999) 'Globalisation, property relations and the history of labour law:

the beginning of a voyage?', in van der Linden, M and Price, R (eds) (1999) *The Rise and Development of Collective Labour Law*, Berne: Peter Lang

Woodiwiss, A (2001a) *The Visual in Social Theory*, London: Athlone

Woodiwiss, M (1988) *Crime, Crusades and Corruption: Prohibitions in the United States, 1900–1987*, London: Pinter

Woodiwiss, M (2001b) *Organised Crime and American Power*, Toronto: University of Toronto Press

World Bank (1995) *World Development Report: Workers in an Integrating World*, Oxford: OUP

Yourow, HC (1995) *The Margin of Appreciation Doctrine in the Dynamics of European Human Rights Jurisprudence*, The Hague: Kluwer

Zhao, D (2001) 'From dreams to reality: rural-urban migration in the Pearl River delta', unpublished PhD thesis, University of Esse

Index

For Product Safety Concerns and Information please contact our EU representative GPSR@taylorandfrancis.com
Taylor & Francis Verlag GmbH, Kaufingerstraße 24, 80331 München, Germany

www.ingramcontent.com/pod-product-compliance
Ingram Content Group UK Ltd.
Pitfield, Milton Keynes, MK11 3LW, UK
UKHW040855180926
475701UK00001B/7

* 9 7 8 1 9 0 4 3 8 5 0 8 0 *